ULTRA EASY DINNERS

Ultra Easy Dinners

13-Digit ISBN: 978-1-64643-294-3
10-Digit ISBN: 1-64643-294-0

This book may be ordered by mail from the publisher. Please include $5.99 for postage and handling. Please support your local bookseller first!

Books published by Cider Mill Press Book Publishers are available at special discounts for bulk purchases in the United States by corporations, institutions, and other organizations. For more information, please contact the publisher.

Cider Mill Press Book Publishers
"Where good books are ready for press"

PO Box 454
12 Spring Street
Kennebunkport, Maine 04046

Visit us online!
cidermillpress.com

Typography: Nobel
Image Credits: Pages 24, 28, 40, 57, 58, 65, 73, 74, 84, 100, 108, 116, 124, 127, 130–131, 133, 142–143, 159, 164–165, 167, 181, 195, 196, 200–201, 204, 207, 222–223, 226, 230–231, and 233 courtesy of Cider Mill Press. All other images used under official license from Shutterstock.com

Back cover image: Chicken Tsukune, page 92
Front endpaper image: Chicken de Champiñones, page 96
Back endpaper image: Chicken Succotash Soup, page 196

Printed in China

1 2 3 4 5 6 7 8 9 0
First Edition

ULTRA EASY DINNERS

100+ Meals in 15 Minutes or Less

CIDER MILL PRESS
BOOK PUBLISHERS
KENNEBUNKPORT, MAINE

CONTENTS

Introduction

AT THE END OF THE DAY, the prospect of dinner can seem daunting. Even before the cooking commences, there's the very real potential of traffic to negotiate on the commute home, grocery shopping to do, and food preparation to push through. Afterward, there's cleanup and dishes. Add it all up, and the better part of an evening has been consumed, leaving little time to relax and recharge for the next day. Faced with all of that, there's a tendency to take the easy way out when the time comes for the day's final meal, either going to a restaurant or reaching for a delivery menu. While dining out occasionally is perfectly fine, making it a go-to will leave your waistline—and your wallet—worse for wear.

If you're thinking there's got to be some other way, some approach that allows you to get something enjoyable on the table without also gobbling up all your free time, you're in luck.

Truth is, there is a quick and easy at-home option for whatever hankering you may have, whether it be the comfort of a carb-laden bowl of noodles, a juicy, perfectly seared steak, or a wholesome and energizing plant-based meal. All that is required is a little bit of planning ahead—a thorough grocery shopping excursion once a week and a well-stocked pantry are both musts—and an open mind. Mashed avocado spread on sourdough toast and seasoned with salt and pepper may not feel like dinner in the traditional, meat-and-potatoes sense, but it is far easier, far tastier, far healthier, and, yes, far quicker. Once you push back from the table 20 minutes after you started cooking, satisfied and ready to indulge in your favorite pastime, you'll start to see dinner as more than just a slog that punctuates the end of each day.

Quick Comfort

Speed is particularly important when you need dinner to supply a bit of relief after an especially trying day, as you simply won't have much energy to devote to meal prep. But that doesn't mean one has to turn to takeout. In truth, there are a host of great options that can carry you home, from classics like tacos and pasta to contemporary-leaning fare like Avocado Toast and Veggie Burgers.

Avocado Toast

YIELD: 4 Servings
ACTIVE TIME: 10 Minutes
TOTAL TIME: 10 Minutes

INGREDIENTS

4 slices of thick-cut bacon

4 thick slices of sourdough bread

Flesh of 2 avocados

¼ cup full-fat Greek yogurt

Salt and pepper, to taste

DIRECTIONS

1. Place the bacon in a large skillet and cook over medium heat until it is crispy, about 8 minutes, turning the bacon as necessary. Transfer to a paper towel-lined plate to drain and cool slightly. When cool enough to handle, chop the bacon into bite-size pieces.

2. Using a toaster or your oven, toast the slices of bread.

3. While the bread is toasting, place the avocados and yogurt in a mixing bowl and stir until combined. Season the mixture with salt and pepper.

4. Spread the avocado mixture on the toast, top with the bacon, and enjoy.

Huevos Rancheros

YIELD: 4 Servings
ACTIVE TIME: 15 Minutes
TOTAL TIME: 15 Minutes

INGREDIENTS

¾ cup extra-virgin olive oil

4 corn tortillas

3 large tomatoes

¼ onion

2 serrano chile peppers, stems and seeds removed, sliced

Salt, to taste

4 eggs

½ cup chopped fresh cilantro, for garnish

½ lb. queso fresco, shredded, for garnish

Black beans, warmed, for serving

DIRECTIONS

1. Place half the olive oil in a large skillet and warm over medium-high heat. Add the tortillas and fry for about 1 minute on each side. Transfer the tortillas to a paper towel–lined plate and let them drain.

2. Place the tomatoes, onion, and chiles in a blender and puree until smooth.

3. Place 2 tablespoons of the remaining olive oil in a small skillet and warm over medium heat. Carefully add the puree, reduce the heat to low, and cook the salsa for 5 minutes. Season with salt and then set the salsa aside.

4. Place the remaining oil in a skillet, add the eggs, season the yolks generously with salt, and cook as desired.

5. To assemble, place an egg on top of a fried tortilla, spoon the salsa on top, and garnish with the cheese and cilantro. Serve with black beans.

Huevos Rancheros, see page 11

Best Burgers Ever

YIELD: 4 Servings
ACTIVE TIME: 15 Minutes
TOTAL TIME: 15 Minutes

INGREDIENTS

1 tablespoon extra-virgin olive oil

1 lb. ground beef (80 percent lean recommended)

1 teaspoon kosher salt

½ teaspoon white pepper

1 egg white

⅓ cup bread crumbs

4 brioche buns

DIRECTIONS

1. Place the olive oil in a cast-iron skillet and warm it over medium heat.
2. Place the remaining ingredients in a bowl and stir until well combined. Divide the mixture into four equal parts and form into patties that are each about 1 inch thick.
3. Place the patties on the grill or in the pan. Cover and cook until browned, about 5 minutes.
4. Flip the patties over, cover the pan, and cook until the desired level of doneness is achieved, 5 to 6 minutes. Remove the burgers from the pan and sandwich them between the buns with your favorite condiments and fixings.

Tacos

YIELD: 4 Servings
ACTIVE TIME: 10 Minutes
TOTAL TIME: 10 Minutes

INGREDIENTS

1 tablespoon extra-virgin olive oil, plus more as needed

1 lb. ground beef

1 tablespoon kosher salt

2 teaspoons cumin

2 teaspoons paprika

1 tablespoon garlic powder

1 teaspoon cayenne pepper

1 teaspoon chili powder

Corn tortillas, for serving

DIRECTIONS

1. Place the oil in a large skillet and warm it over medium-high heat.

2. Add the ground beef and all the seasonings. Cook, breaking up the meat with a wooden spoon, until it is browned and cooked through, about 8 minutes.

3. Serve with the corn tortillas and your favorite taco fixings.

Veggie Burgers

YIELD: 4 Servings
ACTIVE TIME: 15 Minutes
TOTAL TIME: 15 Minutes

INGREDIENTS

1 (14 oz.) can of black beans, drained and rinsed

⅓ cup minced scallions

¼ cup chopped roasted red peppers

¼ cup corn kernels

½ cup panko

1 egg, lightly beaten

2 tablespoons finely chopped fresh cilantro

½ teaspoon cumin

½ teaspoon cayenne pepper

½ teaspoon black pepper

1 teaspoon fresh lime juice

1 tablespoon extra-virgin olive oil

4 brioche buns

DIRECTIONS

1. Place half of the beans, the scallions, and roasted red peppers in a food processor and pulse until the mixture is a thick paste. Transfer to a large bowl.

2. Add the corn, panko, egg, cilantro, cumin, cayenne, black pepper, and lime juice to the bowl and stir to combine. Add the remaining beans and stir vigorously until the mixture holds together.

3. Place a 12-inch cast-iron skillet over medium-high heat and coat the bottom with the olive oil. Form the mixture into four patties. Place them in the pan, cover the skillet, and cook until browned and cooked through, about 5 minutes per side.

4. Remove the burgers from the pan and sandwich them between the buns with your favorite condiments and fixings.

Grilled Cheese

YIELD: 2 Servings
ACTIVE TIME: 10 Minutes
TOTAL TIME: 10 Minutes

INGREDIENTS

2 oz. cheddar cheese, grated

2 oz. Gruyère cheese, grated

4 slices of bread (½ inch thick)

2 tablespoons unsalted butter

DIRECTIONS

1. Place the cheeses in a bowl and stir to combine.
2. Divide the cheese mixture between two slices of the bread. Top with the remaining slices of bread and press down gently.
3. Place 1 tablespoon of the butter in a large skillet and melt it over medium heat. Add the sandwiches to the pan and cook until the bottoms turn golden brown, 3 to 4 minutes, reducing the heat if necessary to keep the toast from burning.
4. Add the remaining butter, flip the sandwiches over, press down on them, and cook until the cheese is completely melted and both sides of the sandwich are golden brown, about 4 minutes. Enjoy immediately.

BLT with Basil Mayo

YIELD: 2 Servings
ACTIVE TIME: 15 Minutes
TOTAL TIME: 15 Minutes

INGREDIENTS

For the Basil Mayonnaise

½ cup mayonnaise

½ cup fresh basil leaves

For the Sandwiches

6 slices of thick-cut bacon, cooked

Salt and pepper, to taste

4 leaves of romaine lettuce

2 ripe tomatoes, sliced

4 slices of bread

DIRECTIONS

1. To prepare the basil mayonnaise, place the mayonnaise and basil in a blender and puree until smooth. Set aside.

2. To begin preparations for the sandwiches, place the bacon in a skillet and cook over medium heat until crispy, about 8 minutes, turning as necessary. Transfer the bacon to a paper towel–lined plate to drain.

3. Spread a layer of the basil mayonnaise on a slice of bread. Top with 3 slices of bacon, a leaf or two of lettuce, and as much tomato as desired. Season with salt and pepper.

4. Slather another piece of bread with the basil mayonnaise and place it on top of the slice of bread with the bacon and vegetables on it. Repeat to construct the second sandwich and enjoy.

Peanut Butter & Bacon Oats

YIELD: 6 Servings
ACTIVE TIME: 15 Minutes
TOTAL TIME: 15 Minutes

INGREDIENTS

2 cups steel-cut oats

6 cups water

1 tablespoon kosher salt

6 slices of thick-cut bacon

6 eggs

¼ cup crunchy peanut butter

DIRECTIONS

1. Place the oats, water, and salt in a saucepan and cook over medium heat until the oats are tender, about 7 minutes.

2. While the oats are cooking, place the bacon in a large cast-iron skillet and cook over medium heat until crispy, about 8 minutes, turning as necessary.

3. Transfer the bacon to a paper towel–lined plate, add the eggs to the skillet, and fry them in the bacon fat. Transfer the eggs to a plate and cover it loosely with aluminum foil to keep warm.

4. Chop the bacon, add it to the oats along with the peanut butter, and stir to incorporate. Ladle the oatmeal into warmed bowls, top each portion with a fried egg, and serve.

Crostini with Pea & Parmesan Spread

YIELD: 6 Servings
ACTIVE TIME: 5 Minutes
TOTAL TIME: 15 Minutes

INGREDIENTS

1 baguette, sliced

2 tablespoons extra-virgin olive oil, plus more to taste

Salt and pepper, to taste

3 cups peas

1 cup water

3 tablespoons pine nuts

1 cup freshly grated Parmesan cheese

1 garlic clove, minced

½ cup fresh mint, chiffonade

DIRECTIONS

1. Preheat the oven to 400°F and bring water to a boil in a medium saucepan. Brush the slices of baguette with the olive oil and place them on a baking sheet. Place in the oven and bake until the slices are golden brown on both sides, about 6 minutes, turning them over halfway through.
2. While the baguette is toasting in the oven, add salt and the peas to the boiling water and cook until the peas are bright green and warmed through, about 2 minutes.
3. Transfer half of the peas to a food processor. Add the water, pine nuts, Parmesan, and garlic and blitz until pureed.
4. Place the puree in a bowl, add the remaining peas and mint, and fold to incorporate. Season the spread with salt and pepper.
5. Remove the crostini from the oven, top them with the spread, season with salt and pepper, and enjoy.

Pork Fried Rice

YIELD: 8 Servings
ACTIVE TIME: 15 Minutes
TOTAL TIME: 15 Minutes

INGREDIENTS

¼ cup avocado oil

1-inch piece of fresh ginger, peeled and minced

2 garlic cloves, minced

3 large eggs

2 cups minced carrots

4 cups leftover white rice

4 scallions, trimmed and chopped

1 cup peas

2 tablespoons soy sauce

1 tablespoon rice vinegar

1 tablespoon fish sauce

1 tablespoon sesame oil

2 cups chopped leftover pork

DIRECTIONS

1. Place the avocado oil in a large cast-iron skillet and it warm over medium-high heat. Add the ginger and garlic and cook, stirring continually, until they just start to brown, about 1 minute.

2. Add the eggs and scramble until the eggs are set, about 2 minutes. Add the carrots, rice, scallions, and peas and stir to incorporate.

3. Add the soy sauce, rice vinegar, fish sauce, sesame oil, and pork and cook, stirring continually, until everything is warmed through, about 5 minutes. Serve immediately.

Spaghetti alla Carbonara

YIELD: 4 Servings
ACTIVE TIME: 15 Minutes
TOTAL TIME: 15 Minutes

INGREDIENTS

2½ tablespoons extra-virgin olive oil

4 oz. pancetta or bacon, diced

Salt and pepper, to taste

2 large eggs, at room temperature

¾ cup freshly grated Parmesan cheese, plus more for garnish

1 lb. spaghetti

DIRECTIONS

1. Bring a large saucepan of water to a boil. Add 2 tablespoons of the olive oil to a large skillet and warm it over medium heat. When the oil starts to shimmer, add the pancetta or bacon, and season it with pepper. Sauté the pancetta or bacon until its fat renders and the meat starts turning golden brown, about 5 minutes. Remove the skillet from heat and cover it partially.

2. Place the eggs in a small bowl and whisk until scrambled. Add the Parmesan, season with salt and pepper, and stir until combined.

3. Add salt and the pasta to the boiling water. Cook 2 minutes short of the directed cooking time, reserve ¼ cup of the pasta water, and drain the pasta.

4. Return the pot to the stove, raise the heat to high, and add the remaining olive oil and the reserved pasta water. Add the drained pasta and toss to combine. Cook until the pasta has absorbed the water.

5. Remove the pot from heat, add the pancetta or bacon and the egg-and-Parmesan mixture, and toss to coat the pasta. Divide the pasta between the serving bowls, season with pepper, and top each portion with additional Parmesan.

Spaghetti with Zucchini & Pesto

YIELD: 4 Servings
ACTIVE TIME: 15 Minutes
TOTAL TIME: 15 Minutes

INGREDIENTS

Salt, to taste

1 lb. spaghetti or fettuccine

3 zucchini, sliced very thin with a mandoline

Pesto (see page 49)

DIRECTIONS

1. Bring a large pot of water to a boil. When it is boiling, add salt and the pasta and cook until it is nearly al dente, about 7 minutes. When the pasta has 1 minute left to cook, add the zucchini, and stir to combine.

2. Reserve ¼ cup of pasta water and then drain the pasta and zucchini. Return them to the pot, add the reserved pasta water, and cook over high heat until all of the water has been absorbed, about 1 minute.

3. Divide the pasta and zucchini between the plates and top each portion with the pesto.

Fettuccine Alfredo

YIELD: 4 Servings
ACTIVE TIME: 15 Minutes
TOTAL TIME: 15 Minutes

INGREDIENTS

Salt and pepper, to taste

¾ lb. fettuccine

½ cup heavy cream

2½ tablespoons unsalted butter, at room temperature

1 cup Parmesan cheese, grated, plus more for garnish

½ teaspoon freshly grated nutmeg

DIRECTIONS

1. Bring a large pot of water to a boil. Once it's boiling, add salt to taste and the fettuccine and cook for 6 minutes. Reserve ½ cup of pasta water and drain the fettuccine.

2. Place the reserved pasta water and heavy cream in a large skillet and bring it to a simmer. Add the butter and stir until it has been emulsified. Gradually incorporate the Parmesan, making sure each addition has melted before adding the next.

3. Add the fettuccine to the skillet and toss to combine. Sprinkle the nutmeg over the top and season with pepper before serving.

Pasta Puttanesca

YIELD: 6 Servings
ACTIVE TIME: 15 Minutes
TOTAL TIME: 15 Minutes

INGREDIENTS

½ cup extra-virgin olive oil

3 garlic cloves, minced

1 (28 oz.) can of peeled whole San Marzano tomatoes, crushed by hand and with their liquid

½ lb. black olives, pits removed

¼ cup nonpareil capers, drained

5 anchovies in olive oil, drained and chopped

1 teaspoon red pepper flakes

Salt and pepper, to taste

1 lb. spaghetti

DIRECTIONS

1. Bring water to a boil in a large saucepan. Place the olive oil in a large, deep skillet and warm it over medium heat. Add the garlic and cook, stirring constantly, until it is fragrant, about 1 minute.
2. Add the tomatoes and their liquid, olives, capers, and anchovies to the skillet and cook, stirring frequently, until the anchovies have dissolved. Stir in the red pepper flakes, season with salt and pepper, stir to combine, and raise the heat to medium. Simmer, stirring occasionally, until the sauce thickens slightly, about 10 minutes.
3. While the sauce is simmering, add salt and the spaghetti to the boiling water and cook until it is al dente, 6 to 8 minutes.
4. Drain the pasta, add it to the sauce, toss to combine, and serve.

Orecchiette with Greens & Potatoes

YIELD: 4 Servings
ACTIVE TIME: 15 Minutes
TOTAL TIME: 15 Minutes

INGREDIENTS

6 tablespoons plus 1 teaspoon extra-virgin olive oil

2 garlic cloves, halved

1 teaspoon nonpareil capers, drained and minced

½ cup green olives, pits removed, minced

⅛ teaspoon cayenne pepper

Salt and pepper, to taste

2 large russet potatoes, peeled and chopped

¾ lb. orecchiette

½ lb. greens

¼ cup grated Pecorino Romano cheese, plus more for garnish

DIRECTIONS

1. Bring water to a boil in a large saucepan. Place 6 tablespoons of the olive oil in a large, deep skillet and warm it over medium heat. Add the garlic, capers, olives, and cayenne to the skillet and cook, stirring frequently, until the garlic starts to brown, about 2 minutes. Discard the garlic and remove the pan from heat.

2. Add salt and the potatoes to the boiling water. When the water returns to a boil, add the pasta and cook until it is just shy of al dente, about 5 minutes. Add the greens 1 minute prior to draining the pasta. Reserve ½ cup of the pasta water, drain, and return the pot to the stove.

3. Set the skillet containing the sauce over medium-high heat. Add reserved pasta water to the pot, raise the heat to high, and add the pasta, potatoes, greens, and the remaining olive oil. Toss until the water has been absorbed. Add the Pecorino and toss until distributed. Season the dish with salt and pepper, garnish with additional Pecorino, and serve.

Pasta Primavera

YIELD: 6 Servings
ACTIVE TIME: 15 Minutes
TOTAL TIME: 15 Minutes

INGREDIENTS

2 tablespoons unsalted butter

1 cup peas

½ lb. asparagus, trimmed and chopped

3 scallions, trimmed and chopped

2 garlic cloves, minced

Salt and pepper, to taste

¾ lb. fettuccine

½ cup full-fat Greek yogurt

$^2/_3$ cup grated Parmesan cheese, plus more for garnish

3 tablespoons chopped fresh parsley, for garnish

2 tablespoons chopped fresh tarragon, for garnish

DIRECTIONS

1. Bring water to a boil in a large saucepan. Place the butter in a large skillet and melt it over medium heat. Add peas, asparagus, scallions, and garlic, season it with salt and pepper, and cook, stirring constantly, until the asparagus is tender, about 4 minutes. Transfer the mixture to a bowl.

2. Place the pasta in the water and cook until it is al dente, about 6 minutes. Drain the pasta and add it to the vegetable mixture.

3. Add the yogurt and Parmesan and toss to combine. Garnish the dish with the parsley and tarragon and enjoy.

American Chop Suey

YIELD: 4 Servings
ACTIVE TIME: 15 Minutes
TOTAL TIME: 15 Minutes

INGREDIENTS

Salt and pepper, to taste

1 lb. elbow macaroni

1 lb. ground beef

1 onion, diced

1 (14 oz.) can of diced tomatoes

DIRECTIONS

1. Bring water to a boil in a large saucepan. Add salt and the macaroni and cook until the macaroni is just shy of al dente, about 7 minutes. Drain and set aside.

2. While the water for the macaroni is coming to a boil, place the beef in a large skillet, season it with salt and pepper, and cook over medium-high heat, breaking the beef up with a fork, until it starts to brown, about 5 minutes. Stir in the onion and cook, stirring frequently, until the beef is cooked through and the onion is translucent, about 3 minutes. Add the tomatoes and cook for about 3 minutes, stirring frequently.

3. Stir the macaroni into the skillet and cook until everything is warmed through. Season with salt and pepper and serve.

From the Garden

Mother Nature is always on your side. But she's really got your back when you need to get something tasty on the table in a hurry. Simply put, she's so good at infusing her products with flavor that there's not much left for you to do. Many times, all that's needed is a knife, a little bit of seasoning, and a few gentle stirs. On top of that ease, your efforts will be rewarded with a fresh, energetic feeling that will allow you to make the most of the remainder of the evening.

Caprese Salad

YIELD: 4 Servings
ACTIVE TIME: 5 Minutes
TOTAL TIME: 5 Minutes

INGREDIENTS

1 lb. in-season heirloom tomatoes, sliced

Salt and pepper, to taste

1 lb. fresh mozzarella cheese, sliced

¼ cup Pesto (see page 49)

Quality extra-virgin olive oil, to taste

DIRECTIONS

1. Season the tomatoes with salt and pepper. While alternating, arrange them and the slices of mozzarella on a platter.

2. Drizzle the pesto and olive oil over the tomatoes and mozzarella and serve.

Pesto

YIELD: 2 Cups
ACTIVE TIME: 10 Minutes
TOTAL TIME: 10 Minutes

INGREDIENTS

2 cups packed fresh basil leaves

1 cup packed fresh baby spinach

2 cups freshly grated Parmesan cheese

¼ cup pine nuts

1 garlic clove

2 teaspoons fresh lemon juice

Salt and pepper, to taste

½ cup extra-virgin olive oil

DIRECTIONS

1. Place all the ingredients, except for the olive oil, in a food processor and pulse until pureed.
2. Transfer the puree to a mixing bowl. While whisking, add the olive oil in a slow stream until it is emulsified.

Rice Bowl with Ginger Dressing

YIELD: 4 Servings
ACTIVE TIME: 10 Minutes
TOTAL TIME: 10 Minutes

DIRECTIONS

1. To begin preparations for the rice bowl, place the oil in a large skillet and warm it over medium-high heat. When the oil starts to shimmer, add the tofu and cook until it is browned all over, turning the pieces as necessary.

2. While the tofu is cooking, prepare the dressing. Place all the ingredients in a blender and puree until smooth.

3. Divide the rice between four bowls. Artfully arrange the tofu, carrots, broccoli sprouts, corn, edamame, and avocados on top of each portion.

4. Top each portion with a pinch of salt and the dressing, garnish with the sesame seeds, and serve.

INGREDIENTS

For the Rice Bowl

1 tablespoon extra-virgin olive oil

1 lb. extra-firm tofu, drained and chopped

2 cups leftover white rice, at room temperature

2 carrots, peeled and grated

1 cup broccoli sprouts

1 cup corn kernels

1 cup edamame

Flesh of 2 avocados, sliced thin

Salt, to taste

Sesame seeds, for garnish

For the Dressing

¼ cup chopped white onion

¼ cup peanut oil

1 tablespoon rice vinegar

1-inch piece of fresh ginger, peeled and grated

1 tablespoon minced celery

1 tablespoon soy sauce

1 teaspoon tomato paste

1½ teaspoons sugar

1 teaspoon fresh lemon juice

½ teaspoon kosher salt

Black pepper, to taste

Garden Sesame Noodles

YIELD: 6 Servings
ACTIVE TIME: 15 Minutes
TOTAL TIME: 15 Minutes

INGREDIENTS

1 lb. Chinese egg noodles

2½ tablespoons toasted sesame oil

2 tablespoons tahini paste

1½ tablespoons smooth peanut butter

¼ cup soy sauce

2 tablespoons rice vinegar

1 tablespoon light brown sugar

2 teaspoons chili garlic sauce, plus more for serving

2-inch piece of fresh ginger, peeled and grated

2 garlic cloves, minced

1 red bell pepper, stem and seeds removed, sliced thin

1 cucumber, peeled, seeded, and sliced thin

1 cup snow peas, trimmed

½ cup chopped roasted peanuts

2 tablespoons sesame seeds, toasted

6 scallions, trimmed and chopped

DIRECTIONS

1. Bring a large pot of water to a boil. Add the noodles and stir for the first minute to prevent any sticking. Cook until tender but still chewy, 2 to 3 minutes. Drain and transfer the noodles to a large bowl. Add ½ tablespoon of the sesame oil and toss to coat to prevent the noodles from sticking together.

2. Place the tahini and peanut butter in a small bowl. Add the soy sauce, vinegar, the remaining sesame oil, the sugar, chili garlic sauce, ginger, and garlic and whisk until combined. Taste and adjust the seasoning according to your preference.

3. Add the sauce to the noodles and toss until evenly distributed. Divide the noodles between six bowls and top with the pepper, cucumber, snow peas, peanuts, sesame seeds, and scallions. Serve with additional chili garlic sauce.

Omelet with Arugula, Ricotta, Sun-Dried Tomatoes & Olives

YIELD: 1 Serving
ACTIVE TIME: 5 Minutes
TOTAL TIME: 10 Minutes

INGREDIENTS

3 eggs

Salt, to taste

1 tablespoon unsalted butter

2 tablespoons ricotta cheese

2 sun-dried tomatoes, sliced

4 olives, pits removed, chopped

1 handful of arugula

DIRECTIONS

1. Crack the eggs into a bowl and whisk until scrambled. Season with salt.

2. Place the butter in a small nonstick skillet and melt over medium heat until it starts to foam. Add the eggs and swirl to coat the entire bottom of the pan. Let the eggs cook for 1 or 2 minutes, until the bottom starts to set.

3. Using a spatula, gently flip the omelet over and immediately place the ricotta, sun-dried tomatoes, and olives in the middle. Cook for 1 minute. Place a handful of arugula on top of the other ingredients and fold the omelet in half. Cook for 30 seconds more and serve.

Spring Pea Soup with Lemon Ricotta

YIELD: 4 Servings
ACTIVE TIME: 15 Minutes
TOTAL TIME: 15 Minutes

INGREDIENTS

12 cups water

1 tablespoon plus 2 teaspoons kosher salt

1 cup ricotta cheese

¼ cup heavy cream

2 tablespoons lemon zest

6 strips of lemon peel

3 cups peas

3 shallots, diced

6 fresh mint leaves, plus more for garnish

DIRECTIONS

1. Place the water and 1 tablespoon of the salt in a saucepan and bring to a boil over medium heat.
2. Place the ricotta, cream, lemon zest, and the remaining salt in a food processor and puree until smooth. Season to taste and set the mixture aside.
3. Add the strips of lemon peel to the saucepan with the peas and shallot. Cook for 2 minutes, until the peas are just cooked through.
4. Drain, making sure to reserve 2 cups of the cooking liquid, and immediately transfer the peas, strips of lemon peel, and shallot to a blender. Add the mint leaves and half the reserved cooking liquid, and puree until the desired consistency is achieved, adding more cooking liquid as needed.
5. Season to taste, ladle into warmed bowls, and place a spoonful of the lemon ricotta into each bowl. Garnish with additional mint and serve immediately, as the brilliant green color starts to fade as the soup cools.

Esquites

YIELD: 4 Servings
ACTIVE TIME: 5 Minutes
TOTAL TIME: 5 Minutes

INGREDIENTS

4 cups canned corn, drained

2 tablespoons unsalted butter

1 jalapeño chile pepper, stem and seeds, diced

2 tablespoons mayonnaise

2 teaspoons garlic powder

3 tablespoons sour cream

¼ teaspoon cayenne pepper

¼ teaspoon chili powder

2 tablespoons feta cheese

2 tablespoons Cotija cheese

2 teaspoons fresh lime juice

½ cup finely chopped fresh cilantro

Salt and pepper, to taste

4 cups lettuce or arugula

DIRECTIONS

1. Place the corn in a large mixing bowl.
2. Add the remaining ingredients one at a time, stirring until it is thoroughly incorporated before adding the next one.
3. Taste, adjust the seasoning as necessary, and enjoy.

Coconut & Cucumber Salad

YIELD: 4 Servings
ACTIVE TIME: 15 Minutes
TOTAL TIME: 15 Minutes

INGREDIENTS

5 large cucumbers, peeled and seeds removed

½ cup shredded unsweetened coconut

Zest and juice of 2 limes

¼ cup coconut milk

1 teaspoon chili garlic sauce, plus more as needed

½-inch piece of fresh ginger, peeled and grated

1 teaspoon sugar

1 teaspoon cumin

1 teaspoon kosher salt, plus more to taste

½ cup roasted peanuts, chopped, for garnish

6 scallions, trimmed and sliced thin, for garnish

DIRECTIONS

1. Quarter each cucumber half and then cut the quarters into long, ⅛-inch-thick strips.
2. Place the coconut, lime juice, coconut milk, chili garlic sauce, ginger, sugar, cumin, and salt in a food processor and blitz until smooth.
3. Place the cucumbers in a large serving bowl. Top with the coconut mixture and toss to coat.
4. Sprinkle the lime zest, peanuts, and scallions on top of the dressed noodles, season to taste, and enjoy.

Kuku Sabzi

YIELD: 4 Servings
ACTIVE TIME: 15 Minutes
TOTAL TIME: 15 Minutes

INGREDIENTS

4 eggs

1 teaspoon cumin

1 teaspoon black pepper

1 teaspoon kosher salt

5 scallions, trimmed and sliced thin

1 cup chopped fresh parsley

1 cup chopped fresh cilantro

1 cup chopped fresh dill

2 tablespoons avocado oil

DIRECTIONS

1. In a large bowl, whisk the eggs until smooth. Add the remaining ingredients, except for the oil, and whisk until incorporated.
2. Place the avocado oil in a medium nonstick skillet and warm it over medium-low heat. Pour the egg mixture into the pan and let it cook for 1 minute.
3. Reduce the heat to low, cover the pan, and cook until the frittata begins to set and the bottom is lightly golden brown, about 6 minutes. Flip the frittata using a spatula (or slide it onto a plate and invert it back into the pan) and cook until it is completely set, about 2 minutes more.
4. Transfer the frittata to a platter, slice, and enjoy.

Kuku Sabzi, see page 61

Panzanella

YIELD: 4 Servings
ACTIVE TIME: 15 Minutes
TOTAL TIME: 15 Minutes

INGREDIENTS

6 tablespoons extra-virgin olive oil

4 cups cubed crusty bread

Salt and pepper, to taste

2 tablespoons red wine vinegar

2 tablespoons chopped fresh basil

2 tablespoons chopped fresh oregano

1 lb. cherry tomatoes, halved

1 (14 oz.) can of cannellini beans, drained and rinsed

½ red onion, sliced thin

4 cups baby arugula

Parmesan cheese, shaved, for garnish

DIRECTIONS

1. Place 2 tablespoons of the olive oil in a skillet and warm it over medium-high heat. Add the bread, season it with salt and pepper, and cook, stirring frequently, until it is browned, about 4 minutes. Remove the pan from heat and set it aside.

2. Place the vinegar in a salad bowl. While whisking, slowly drizzle in the remaining olive oil. As this is a split vinaigrette, the oil will not emulsify. Add the herbs, tomatoes, beans, and onion to the vinaigrette and toss to coat.

3. Add the bread and baby arugula to the salad bowl, stir gently until combined, and season the salad with salt and pepper. Garnish with the Parmesan and enjoy.

Onion Bhaji

YIELD: 4 Servings
ACTIVE TIME: 15 Minutes
TOTAL TIME: 15 Minutes

INGREDIENTS

2 eggs

3 large red onions, sliced into thin half-moons

1 cup all-purpose flour

1 teaspoon coriander

1 teaspoon cumin

1 serrano chile pepper, stems and seeds removed, minced

½ teaspoon kosher salt

1 cup canola oil, plus more as needed

DIRECTIONS

1. Place the eggs in a bowl and whisk until scrambled. Add the onions, flour, coriander, cumin, serrano pepper, and salt and stir to combine.

2. Place the canola oil in a medium cast-iron skillet and warm it over medium heat. Add a large spoonful of the onion batter and fry until golden brown, about 30 seconds.

3. Turn the fritter over and fry until it is crisp and golden brown all over, about 30 seconds. Transfer the fritter to a paper towel–lined plate to drain. Repeat with the remaining batter, adding more canola oil if the level gets too low. When all the fritters have been cooked, serve immediately.

Peppers Stuffed with Greek Salad

YIELD: 4 Servings
ACTIVE TIME: 15 Minutes
TOTAL TIME: 15 Minutes

INGREDIENTS

4 yellow bell peppers, seeds removed, halved

12 cherry tomatoes, halved

2 garlic cloves, minced

2 tablespoons extra-virgin olive oil

½ cup crumbled feta cheese

1 cup black olives, pits removed

Salt and pepper, to taste

Leaves from 1 bunch of fresh basil

DIRECTIONS

1. Preheat the oven to 375°F and place the peppers on a parchment-lined baking sheet.

2. Place the cherry tomatoes, garlic, olive oil, feta, and black olives in a mixing bowl and stir to combine. Divide the mixture between the peppers, place them in the oven, and roast until the peppers start to collapse, about 10 minutes.

3. Remove the peppers from the oven, season them with salt and pepper, top with the basil leaves, and enjoy.

Miso Ramen

YIELD: 4 Servings
ACTIVE TIME: 15 Minutes
TOTAL TIME: 15 Minutes

INGREDIENTS

¼ cup sesame seeds

2 tablespoons sesame oil

4 garlic cloves, minced

2-inch piece of fresh ginger, peeled and grated

2 shallots, minced

2 teaspoons chili garlic sauce

6 tablespoons white miso paste

2 tablespoons sugar

2 tablespoons sake

8 cups vegetable stock

½ lb. ramen noodles

Salt and pepper, to taste

Bean sprouts, for garnish

DIRECTIONS

1. Bring water to a boil in a medium saucepan. Place the sesame seeds in a dry skillet and toast over medium heat until browned, about 2 minutes. Remove from the pan and use a mortar and pestle to grind them into a paste, adding water as needed.

2. Place the sesame oil in a large saucepan and warm over medium heat. Add the garlic, ginger, and shallots and cook, stirring continually, for 1 minute.

3. Raise the heat to medium-high and add the chili garlic sauce, miso, sugar, sake, and stock and stir to combine. Bring to a boil, reduce heat so that the broth simmers, and season with salt and pepper. Simmer for about 5 minutes and remove from heat.

4. While the soup is simmering, add the noodles to the boiling water and cook until just tender, about 2 minutes. Drain the noodles and place them in warmed bowls. Pour the broth over the noodles and top each portion with bean sprouts.

Fava Bean Soup

YIELD: 4 Servings
ACTIVE TIME: 10 Minutes
TOTAL TIME: 10 Minutes

INGREDIENTS

5 tablespoons extra-virgin olive oil

1 shallot, minced

4 garlic cloves, minced

6 cups Chicken Stock (see page 151)

1 (14 oz.) can of fava beans, drained and rinsed

Zest and juice of 1 lemon

2 tablespoons finely chopped fresh parsley

½ lb. Halloumi cheese, cut into 4 pieces

Salt and pepper, to taste

Lemon wedges, for serving

DIRECTIONS

1. Place ¼ cup of the olive oil in a skillet and warm it over medium heat. Add the shallot and garlic and cook, stirring continually, until the shallot is translucent, about 3 minutes.

2. Transfer the mixture to a food processor, add the stock, fava beans, lemon zest, lemon juice, and parsley and blitz until the mixture is smooth.

3. Place the puree in a saucepan and warm it over medium heat.

4. While the soup is warming, warm a cast-iron skillet over medium heat. Place the remaining olive oil in a small bowl, add the cheese, and toss to coat. Place the cheese in the pan and cook until browned on both sides, about 2 minutes per side.

5. Season the soup with salt and pepper, ladle it into warmed bowls, and serve the grilled Halloumi and lemon wedges alongside.

Shaved Snap Pea Salad

YIELD: 2 Servings
ACTIVE TIME: 10 Minutes
TOTAL TIME: 10 Minutes

INGREDIENTS

1 lb. snap peas

1 tablespoon chopped fresh dill

1 tablespoon chopped fresh basil

1 tablespoon chopped fresh mint

2 teaspoons honey

¼ cup white vinegar

1 teaspoon kosher salt

1 tablespoon crushed walnuts

DIRECTIONS

1. Using a sharp knife, stack 4 snap peas and cut them into thin slices on a bias. Transfer them to a bowl and repeat with the remaining snap peas.

2. Add the remaining ingredients, toss until well combined, and enjoy.

Edamame Succotash

YIELD: 4 to 6 Servings
ACTIVE TIME: 5 Minutes
TOTAL TIME: 15 Minutes

INGREDIENTS

4 slices of thick-cut bacon

2 tablespoons unsalted butter

1 red onion, minced

4 cups canned corn

1 red bell pepper, stem and seeds removed, diced

2 cups edamame

Salt and pepper, to taste

1 tablespoon chopped fresh marjoram

¼ cup chopped fresh basil

DIRECTIONS

1. Place a large skillet over medium heat, add the bacon, and cook until crispy, about 8 minutes, turning it as necessary. Remove from the pan and place on a paper towel–lined plate to drain. When it is cool enough to handle, crumble into bite-sized pieces.
2. While the bacon is cooking, place the butter in a large skillet and melt it over medium-high heat. Add the onion and cook, stirring occasionally, until it is translucent, about 3 minutes.
3. Add the corn, bell pepper, and edamame and cook, stirring frequently, until the corn is tender, about 3 minutes.
4. Season the mixture with salt and pepper, stir in the marjoram, basil, and crumbled bacon, and enjoy.

Ful Medames

YIELD: 4 Servings
ACTIVE TIME: 15 Minutes
TOTAL TIME: 15 Minutes

INGREDIENTS

1 tablespoon avocado oil

1 onion, chopped

3 garlic cloves, minced

2 tomatoes, chopped

2 (14 oz.) cans of fava beans, drained and rinsed

1 teaspoon cumin

1 tablespoon ras el hanout

¼ teaspoon cayenne pepper

3 tablespoons fresh lemon juice

¼ cup fresh parsley, chopped

Salt, to taste

DIRECTIONS

1. Place the avocado oil in a large skillet and warm it over medium heat. Add the onion and garlic and cook, stirring frequently, until the onion is translucent, about 3 minutes.

2. Add the tomatoes and cook for 2 minutes, stirring occasionally. Stir in the fava beans, cumin, ras el hanout, and cayenne pepper and cook for 6 minutes.

3. Remove the pan from the heat and mash the fava beans lightly, right in the skillet, until most of the beans are mashed. Scoop into a serving bowl, stir in the lemon juice and parsley, season with salt, and enjoy.

Ful Medames, see page 77

For the Meat Lovers

Just because you don't have time to braise a pork shoulder or roast a chicken doesn't mean that you can't indulge your carnivorous side on those nights where you're looking to get through dinner quickly. In fact, a brief spell in a pan over high heat is your best friend when you need to soothe such a craving, as this method is your best bet to supply the various textures that set the imagination and taste buds alight. Whether it be beef, lamb, chicken, or pork, an easy solution lies within.

Sukiyaki

YIELD: 4 Servings
ACTIVE TIME: 15 Minutes
TOTAL TIME: 15 Minutes

INGREDIENTS

Salt, to taste

1½ lbs. udon noodles

1 tablespoon extra-virgin olive oil

3 tablespoons brown sugar

2 lbs. rib eye, sliced very thin

½ cup mirin

½ cup sake

⅓ cup soy sauce

1 cup water

1 bunch of scallions, trimmed and sliced

2 cups chopped napa cabbage

4 oz. shiitake mushrooms, chopped

1 cup fresh spinach

½ lb. tofu, drained and diced

DIRECTIONS

1. Bring salted water to a boil in a Dutch oven. Add the noodles to the boiling water and cook for 2 minutes. Drain, rinse with cold water, and set the noodles aside.

2. Place the oil in the Dutch oven and warm over medium-high heat. When the oil starts to shimmer, add the brown sugar and rib eye and cook, while turning, until the steak is browned all over, about 2 minutes. Add the mirin, sake, soy sauce, and water and stir to combine.

3. Carefully arrange the noodles, scallions, cabbage, mushrooms, spinach, and tofu in the broth. Cover and steam until the cabbage is wilted, about 5 minutes. Ladle into warmed bowls and enjoy immediately.

Pan-Seared Rib Eye

YIELD: 2 Servings
ACTIVE TIME: 15 Minutes
TOTAL TIME: 15 Minutes

INGREDIENTS

1 lb. rib eye steak

2 teaspoons kosher salt

2 tablespoons canola oil

4 tablespoons unsalted butter

2 sprigs of fresh rosemary

DIRECTIONS

1. Pat the steak dry and then season both sides of the steak with salt.

2. Place the canola oil in a cast-iron skillet and warm it over medium-high heat. Place the steak in the pan and cook it until that side has a nice sear on it, 4 to 5 minutes.

3. Flip the steak over, add 2 tablespoons of butter to the pan, tilt the pan slightly, and spoon the butter and pan juices over the top of the steak.

4. Cook the steak for another 3 to 4 minutes, or until the desired doneness is achieved. Just before removing the steak from the pan, add the remaining butter and rosemary, tilt the pan slightly, and spoon the butter and pan juices over the steak. Remove the steak from the pan and let it rest on a cutting board for 2 minutes before serving.

Chipotle T-Bone

YIELD: 2 Servings
ACTIVE TIME: 15 Minutes
TOTAL TIME: 15 Minutes

INGREDIENTS

1 tablespoon chipotle chile powder

2 teaspoons kosher salt

2 tablespoons extra-virgin olive oil

1 lb. T-bone steak

4 tablespoons unsalted butter

DIRECTIONS

1. Prepare your gas grill for high heat (about 500°F).
2. In a small bowl, combine the chipotle chile powder, salt, and olive oil. Pat the steak dry and then generously apply the chipotle mixture to both sides of the steak.
3. Place the steak over a hot part of the grill—a section you can only leave your hand over for 2 seconds before you need to move it away—and cook until nicely seared, about 5 minutes.
4. Flip the steak over, brush the top with some of the butter and cook for about 3 minutes, or until the desired level of doneness is achieved.
5. Remove the steak from the grill, brush it with butter, and let it rest for 2 minutes before enjoying.

Lamb Chops

YIELD: 4 Servings
ACTIVE TIME: 15 Minutes
TOTAL TIME: 15 Minutes

INGREDIENTS

4 garlic cloves, minced

½ cup fresh rosemary, finely chopped

¼ cup extra-virgin olive oil, plus more to taste

2¼ lbs. lamb chops, pounded thin and trimmed

Salt and pepper, to taste

DIRECTIONS

1. Warm a large cast-iron skillet over medium-high heat.
2. Place the garlic, rosemary, and olive oil in a large bowl and stir to combine. Set the mixture aside.
3. Season the lamb chops with salt and pepper, add them to the marinade, and turn them until evenly coated.
4. Place the lamb chops in the pan and cook until well seared on both sides and medium-rare, about 3 minutes per side. Transfer the lamb chops to a platter and let them rest for 2 minutes before serving.

Lamb Chops, see page 87

Veal Scallopini

YIELD: 4 Servings
ACTIVE TIME: 10 Minutes
TOTAL TIME: 15 Minutes

INGREDIENTS

½ cup all-purpose flour

½ teaspoon nutmeg

Salt and pepper, to taste

2 tablespoons unsalted butter

1 lb. veal cutlets, pounded thin

½ cup Beef Stock (see page 210)

¼ cup sliced green olives

Zest and juice of 1 lemon

DIRECTIONS

1. Warm a large cast-iron skillet over medium heat for 2 minutes.

2. Place the flour, nutmeg, salt, and pepper on a large plate and stir to combine.

3. Place the butter in the pan. When it starts to sizzle, dredge the veal in the seasoned flour until coated lightly on both sides. Working in batches, place the veal in the skillet and cook for about 1 minute on each side, until it is browned and the juices run clear. Set the cooked veal aside.

4. Deglaze the pan with the stock. Add the olives, lemon zest, and lemon juice, stir to combine, and cook until heated through.

5. To serve, plate the veal and pour the pan sauce over each cutlet.

Chicken Tsukune

YIELD: 4 to 6 Servings
ACTIVE TIME: 15 Minutes
TOTAL TIME: 15 Minutes

INGREDIENTS

2 lbs. chicken thighs, ground

1 large egg, lightly beaten

1 cup panko

2 teaspoons miso paste

2 tablespoons sake

1½ tablespoons mirin

½ teaspoon black pepper

Teriyaki sauce, to taste

1½ scallions, sliced, for garnish

Sesame seeds, for garnish

DIRECTIONS

1. Place the ground chicken, egg, panko, miso, sake, mirin, and the pepper in a bowl and stir to combine. Form the mixture into compact pieces that are round or oblong.
2. Warm a cast-iron grill pan over high heat and lightly coat the pan with nonstick cooking spray.
3. Add the meatballs and cook until they start to brown, about 5 minutes. Turn them and cook until they are completely cooked through, about 5 minutes. Remove from the grill and lightly baste the cooked meatballs with some teriyaki sauce.
4. Garnish the meatballs with the sesame seeds and scallions and serve with additional teriyaki sauce.

Spicy Tonkatsu

YIELD: 4 Servings
ACTIVE TIME: 15 Minutes
TOTAL TIME: 15 Minutes

INGREDIENTS

1½ lbs. pork cutlets

¼ cup wasabi paste

¼ cup extra-virgin olive oil

2 tablespoons horseradish

1 tablespoon chopped fresh parsley

2 tablespoons finely chopped fresh chives

Salt and pepper, to taste

2 cups panko

Lemon wedges, for serving

DIRECTIONS

1. Preheat the broiler on your oven. Pat the cutlets dry and lightly coat each one with the wasabi paste. In a bowl, combine 2 tablespoons of the olive oil, the horseradish, parsley, chives, salt, and pepper. Add the panko and carefully stir to coat. Set the seasoned panko aside.

2. Place a large cast-iron skillet over medium heat and coat the bottom with the remaining olive oil. Add the pork cutlets and cook until golden brown, about 4 minutes. Flip the cutlets over and cook until golden brown on the other side, another 4 minutes.

3. Remove the cutlets from the skillet and dip each one into the seasoned panko until completely coated. Return the coated cutlets to the skillet.

4. While keeping a close watch on the breaded cutlets, place the pan under the broiler. Broil, turning the cutlets over once, until the breading is browned and crispy. Slice thin and serve with the lemon wedges.

Chicken de Champiñones

YIELD: 4 Servings
ACTIVE TIME: 15 Minutes
TOTAL TIME: 15 Minutes

INGREDIENTS

2 tablespoons extra-virgin olive oil

1 lb. chicken cutlets

Salt and pepper, to taste

6 button mushrooms, quartered

1 shallot, chopped

1 garlic clove, sliced

¼ cup white wine

¼ cup heavy cream

¼ cup shredded Oaxaca cheese

1 teaspoon cumin

Fresh cilantro, chopped, for garnish

DIRECTIONS

1. Place the olive oil in a skillet and warm it over medium-high heat. Season the chicken with salt and pepper, place it in the pan, and sear for 1 minute on each side.

2. Add the mushrooms and cook for about 30 seconds. Add the shallot and garlic and cook for another 30 seconds, stirring frequently.

3. Deglaze the pan with the white wine and cook until the liquid has reduced by half. Stir in the heavy cream, Oaxaca cheese, and cumin and cook until chicken is cooked through, about 6 minutes.

4. Garnish with the cilantro and enjoy.

Pork Milanesa

YIELD: 4 Servings
ACTIVE TIME: 15 Minutes
TOTAL TIME: 15 Minutes

INGREDIENTS

2 cups bread crumbs

4 large eggs

1 cup extra-virgin olive oil

2 lbs. pork cutlets (¼ inch thick)

Salt, to taste

DIRECTIONS

1. Place the bread crumbs in a shallow bowl. Place the eggs in a separate bowl and beat until scrambled.

2. Place the olive oil in a large, deep skillet and warm it over medium-high heat until it is hot enough that a bread crumb sizzles gently when added.

3. Season the pork cutlets with salt, dredge them in the beaten eggs, and then in the bread crumbs until they are coated all over. Gently press down on the bread crumbs so that they adhere to the pork.

4. Slip the cutlets into the hot oil and fry until golden brown on both sides and cooked through, 8 to 10 minutes. Transfer the milanesa to a paper towel-lined plate to drain and enjoy.

Filet Mignon with Peppercorn Cream Sauce

YIELD: 2 Servings
ACTIVE TIME: 6 Minutes
TOTAL TIME: 15 Minutes

INGREDIENTS

2 tablespoons canola oil

2 tablespoons peppercorns

1 cup heavy cream

Salt, to taste

1 lb. filet mignon

2 tablespoons unsalted butter

Fresh rosemary, chopped, for garnish

DIRECTIONS

1. Place the canola oil in a large cast-iron skillet and warm it over high heat.

2. Using a mortar and pestle or a spice grinder, roughly grind the peppercorns. Place them in a separate large skillet and toast for 1 minute. Add the cream and a pinch of salt and reduce the heat to medium-low and cook, stirring constantly, for 2 minutes. Remove the pan from heat and set it aside.

3. Season the steaks with salt, place them in the cast-iron skillet, and cook until they are well seared, about 4 minutes.

4. Flip the steaks over, add the butter to the pan, tilt the pan slightly, and spoon the butter-and-oil mixture over the top of the steaks. Cook the steaks until they have reached the desired level of doneness, 3 to 4 minutes.

5. Transfer the steaks to a plate, spoon the sauce over the top, garnish with rosemary, and enjoy.

Lamb, Szechuan Style

YIELD: 4 Servings
ACTIVE TIME: 15 Minutes
TOTAL TIME: 15 Minutes

INGREDIENTS

3 tablespoons cumin seeds

2 teaspoons Szechuan peppercorns

1 teaspoon kosher salt

3 tablespoons canola oil

4 dried red chile peppers, stems and seeds removed, torn

2 teaspoons red pepper flakes

1½ lbs. boneless leg of lamb, cubed

1 yellow onion, sliced

2 scallions, trimmed and sliced thin, for garnish

Fresh cilantro, chopped, for garnish

White rice, cooked, for serving

DIRECTIONS

1. Place the cumin seeds and Szechuan peppercorns in a large, dry cast-iron skillet and toast over medium heat for 1 minute. Remove the mixture from the pan and grind to a fine powder with a mortar and pestle.

2. Place the salt, 2 tablespoons of the canola oil, the dried chilies, red pepper flakes, and toasted spice mixture in a large bowl and stir to combine. Add the lamb pieces and toss until they are coated.

3. Add the remaining canola oil to the large cast-iron skillet and warm it over high heat. Add the lamb and onion and cook, stirring occasionally, until the lamb is browned all over and medium-rare, 6 to 8 minutes.

4. Garnish the dish with scallions and cilantro and serve it with white rice.

Chicken Livers with Marsala

YIELD: 4 Servings
ACTIVE TIME: 10 Minutes
TOTAL TIME: 10 Minutes

INGREDIENTS

1 teaspoon extra-virgin olive oil

2 tablespoons unsalted butter

1 yellow onion, sliced into half-moons

1 lb. chicken livers, cleaned

¼ cup sweet Marsala wine

1 mandarin orange, peeled and cut into segments

DIRECTIONS

1. Place the olive oil and butter in a large cast-iron skillet and warm the mixture over medium heat. Add the onion and cook, stirring occasionally, until it is translucent, about 3 minutes.
2. Place the onion on one side of the skillet and place the chicken livers on the other. Cook the chicken livers until they are lightly browned on both sides, about 2 minutes per side. Do not stir the onions.
3. Raise the heat to high and carefully add the wine. Let it boil for 1 minute so that the alcohol gets cooked off. Add the mandarin segments, stir to coat, and cook until they are ready to burst, about 1 minute. Serve immediately.

Thai Basil Chicken

YIELD: 4 Servings
ACTIVE TIME: 15 Minutes
TOTAL TIME: 15 Minutes

INGREDIENTS

¼ cup fish sauce

¼ cup soy sauce

2 tablespoons water

2 tablespoons brown sugar

4 boneless, skinless chicken breasts, chopped

2 tablespoons canola oil

3 shallots, sliced thin

2 red bell peppers, stems and seeds removed, sliced thin

2 fresh red bird's eye chili peppers, stems and seeds removed, sliced thin

3 garlic cloves, chopped

1½ cups fresh Thai basil

DIRECTIONS

1. Place the fish sauce, soy sauce, water, and sugar in a bowl and stir to combine. Set half the mixture aside, add the chicken, and let the chicken marinate.

2. Place the canola oil in a large cast-iron skillet and warm over medium-high heat. Add the shallots, bell peppers, chilies, and garlic and cook, stirring continually, for 2 minutes.

3. Remove the chicken from the marinade and add the chicken to the pan. Cook, stirring frequently, until it is almost cooked through, about 5 minutes.

4. Add the reserved mixture and cook for another minute.

5. Remove the pan from heat and stir in 1 cup of the basil. Serve immediately and top each portion with some of the remaining Thai basil leaves.

Fruits of the Sea

If you're adamant about getting dinner on the table quickly, but not the biggest fan of seafood, you need to change your perspective. Simply put, the incredible bounty provided by the world's oceans is the best friend of the time-sensitive cook, as seafood's famed freshness and light character requires very little time and effort to become toothsome.

Pub Sardines

YIELD: 1 Serving
ACTIVE TIME: 10 Minutes
TOTAL TIME: 10 Minutes

INGREDIENTS

1 tablespoon sake

1 tablespoon soy sauce

1 can of sardines in olive oil, drained

Pinch of black pepper

2 teaspoons sansho peppercorns

Crusty bread, for serving

DIRECTIONS

1. Add the sake and soy sauce to the can of sardines.
2. Top with the black pepper and sansho peppercorns.
3. Place the can directly on a burner on your stove, cook over the lowest heat for 4 to 5 minutes, and serve with bread.

Garlic Shrimp

YIELD: 4 Servings
ACTIVE TIME: 10 Minutes
TOTAL TIME: 10 Minutes

INGREDIENTS

4 tablespoons unsalted butter, softened

1 lb. shrimp, shells removed, deveined

8 garlic cloves, minced

½ teaspoon lemon-pepper seasoning

1 tablespoon fresh lemon juice

1 tablespoon minced fresh chives or parsley, for garnish

DIRECTIONS

1. Place a medium cast-iron skillet over medium heat and add the butter.
2. When the butter has melted and is foaming, add the shrimp and cook, without stirring, for 3 minutes. Remove the shrimp from the pan with a slotted spoon and set them aside.
3. Reduce the heat to medium-low and add the garlic and lemon-pepper seasoning. Cook until the garlic has softened, about 3 minutes.
4. Return the shrimp to the pan and cooked until warmed through, about 1 minute. To serve, sprinkle the lemon juice over the top of the shrimp and garnish with the chives or parsley.

Crab & Okra Soup

YIELD: 4 Servings
ACTIVE TIME: 15 Minutes
TOTAL TIME: 15 Minutes

INGREDIENTS

½ cup coconut oil

10 okra pods, sliced into ½-inch rounds

1 red bell pepper, stem and seeds removed, diced

1 yellow onion, sliced into half-moons

1 habanero pepper, stem and seeds removed, chopped

1 large potato, peeled and diced

4 cups vegetable stock

1 cup clam juice

1 cup coconut milk

Salt, to taste

1 cup peanuts, chopped

4 cups fresh spinach leaves

1 lb. lump crabmeat

Lime wedges, for serving

DIRECTIONS

1. Place the coconut oil in the Dutch oven and warm over medium heat. When it starts to shimmer, add the okra, bell pepper, onion, habanero pepper, and potato and cook, stirring frequently, until the onion starts to soften, about 5 minutes.
2. Add the stock and clam juice, bring to a simmer, and cook for 5 minutes. Stir in the coconut milk, return to a simmer, and season with salt.
3. Transfer the soup to a blender and puree until smooth. Return the soup to the Dutch oven, stir in the peanuts, spinach, and crabmeat and cook until the spinach has wilted, about 2 minutes.
4. Ladle the soup into warmed bowls and serve with lime wedges.

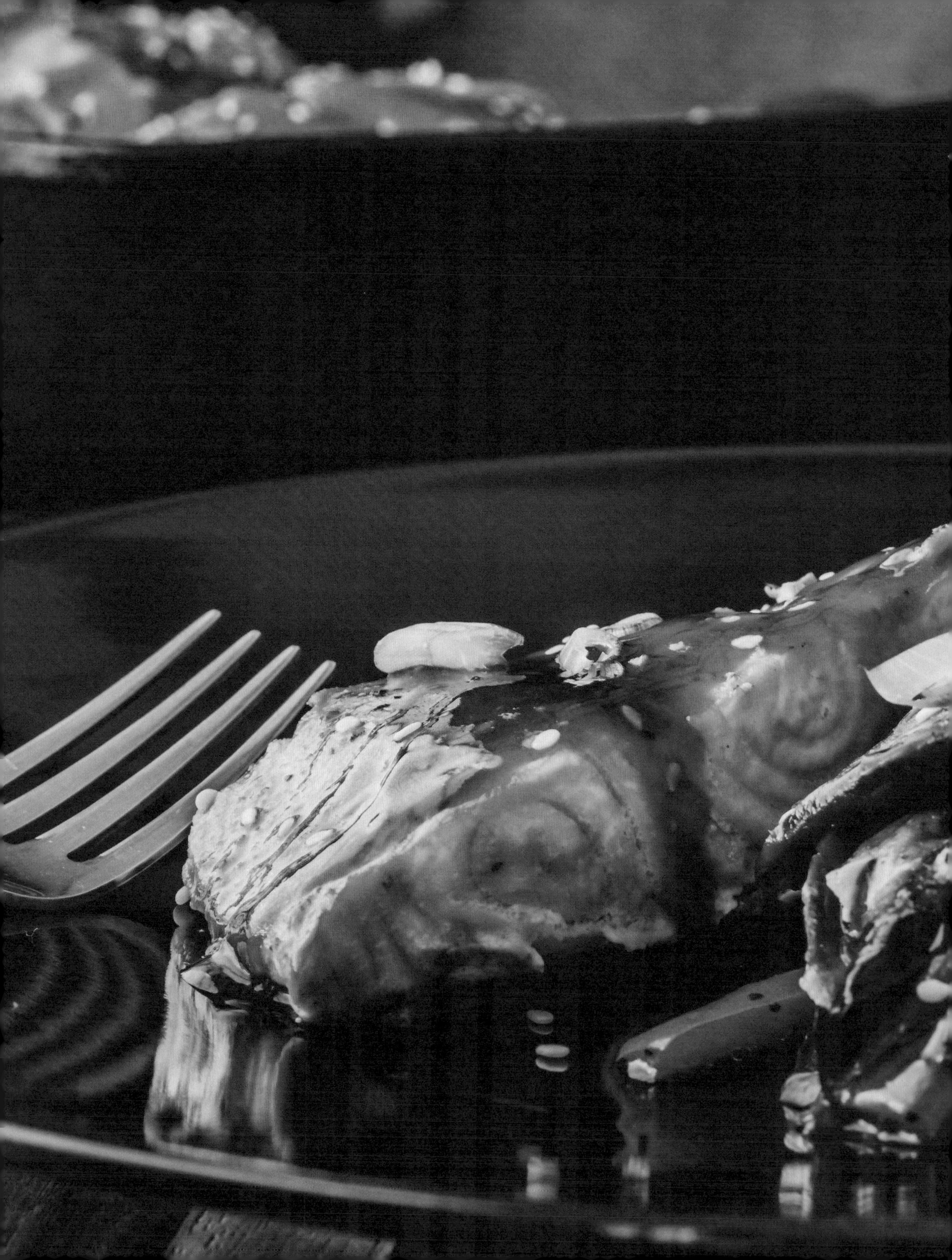

Teriyaki Salmon with Vegetables

YIELD: 4 Servings
ACTIVE TIME: 5 Minutes
TOTAL TIME: 15 Minutes

INGREDIENTS

3 tablespoons extra-virgin olive oil

4 Chinese eggplants, sliced into ½-inch pieces

1 red bell pepper, stem and seeds removed, sliced thin

2 tablespoons chopped scallions

1 cup bean sprouts

4 salmon fillets, deboned

Salt and pepper, to taste

¼ cup teriyaki sauce

DIRECTIONS

1. Preheat the oven to 375°F. Place the olive oil in the skillet and warm over medium-high heat. Add the eggplants, bell pepper, and scallions to the pan and cook, stirring occasionally, until the eggplants start to break down, about 5 minutes. Add the bean sprouts and stir to incorporate.

2. Place the salmon on top of the vegetables, skin side down, season with salt, pepper, and some of the teriyaki sauce, and transfer the pan to the oven. Bake until the salmon is cooked through, about 8 minutes.

3. Remove the pan from the oven, drizzle the remaining teriyaki sauce over the top, and serve.

Smoked Trout Tostadas

YIELD: 4 Servings
ACTIVE TIME: 15 Minutes
TOTAL TIME: 15 Minutes

INGREDIENTS

½ cup extra-virgin olive oil, plus more as needed

1 large white onion, sliced thin

4 garlic cloves, sliced

1 lb. smoked trout, shredded

2 teaspoons achiote powder

½ lb. carrots, peeled and grated

½ cup shredded cabbage

2 tablespoons chopped Castelvetrano olives

2 tablespoons fresh lemon juice

2 tablespoons kosher salt

4 corn tortillas

DIRECTIONS

1. Place the olive oil in a large skillet and warm it over medium-high heat.

2. While the olive oil is warming up, coat another skillet with olive oil and warm it over medium heat. Add the onion and garlic and cook, stirring frequently, until the onion is translucent, about 3 minutes.

3. Stir the trout and achiote into the onion mixture and cook, stirring to break up the trout, until warmed through, about 3 minutes. Remove the pan from heat, stir in all of the remaining ingredients, except for the tortillas, and let the mixture sit.

4. Add the tortillas to the hot oil and fry until they are crispy, 2 to 3 minutes. Transfer the tostadas to a paper towel–lined plate to drain.

5. Top each tostada with some of the smoked trout mixture and enjoy.

Red Snapper with Tomatillo Sauce

YIELD: 4 Servings
ACTIVE TIME: 10 Minutes
TOTAL TIME: 10 Minutes

INGREDIENTS

1 lb. tomatillos, husked, rinsed, and quartered

½ white onion, chopped

1 serrano pepper, stem removed

1 garlic clove, crushed

1 bunch of fresh cilantro, some leaves reserved for garnish

2 tablespoons extra-virgin olive oil

1½ lbs. skinless red snapper fillets, deboned

Radish, sliced, for garnish

Corn tortillas, for serving

Lime wedges, for serving

DIRECTIONS

1. Place a dry skillet over high heat and add the tomatillos, onion, and serrano pepper. Cook until the tomatillos and pepper are charred slightly, about 3 minutes, and then transfer the vegetables to a blender. Add the garlic and cilantro and puree until smooth.

2. Place the olive oil in a large cast-iron skillet and warm it over medium-high heat. When the oil starts to shimmer, add the red snapper fillets in a single layer and cook until lightly browned, 3 to 4 minutes. Do not turn them over.

3. Remove the pan from heat. Carefully pour the tomatillo sauce over the fish. It will immediately start to simmer. Place the skillet over medium heat and let it simmer until the fish is cooked through, about 4 minutes. Garnish with the reserved cilantro and sliced radish and serve with the tortillas and lime wedges.

Garlic & Lime Calamari

YIELD: 4 Servings
ACTIVE TIME: 10 Minutes
TOTAL TIME: 10 Minutes

INGREDIENTS

1½ lbs. squid, sliced into rings

2 tablespoons extra-virgin olive oil

1 tablespoon unsalted butter

10 garlic cloves, chopped

3 tablespoons white wine

Juice of 1½ limes

Salt and pepper, to taste

Pinch of cayenne pepper

3 tablespoons chopped fresh dill

DIRECTIONS

1. Pat the calamari dry and set it aside. Place the olive oil and butter in a large cast-iron skillet and warm the mixture over medium-high heat. When the butter starts to foam, add the garlic and cook, stirring continuously, until fragrant, about 1 minute.

2. Add the calamari to the pan, cook for 2 minutes, and then stir in the wine and lime juice. Cook for another 30 seconds, until warmed through, and remove the pan from heat.

3. Season with salt and pepper, stir in the cayenne and dill, and enjoy.

Chilled Calamari Salad

YIELD: 4 to 6 Servings
ACTIVE TIME: 15 Minutes
TOTAL TIME: 15 Minutes

INGREDIENTS

Salt and pepper, to taste

1½ lbs. small squid, bodies and tentacles separated, rinsed well

3 tablespoons red wine vinegar

2 tablespoons harissa sauce

1½ teaspoons Dijon mustard

⅓ cup extra-virgin olive oil

2 oranges, peeled and cut into segments

1 red bell pepper, stem and seeds removed, cut into strips

2 celery stalks, chopped

¼ cup hazelnuts

¼ cup shredded fresh mint

DIRECTIONS

1. Bring approximately 8 cups of water to a boil in a large saucepan and prepare an ice bath. Season the boiling water generously with salt, add the tentacles of the squid, and cook for 1 minute. Add the bodies, cook for another minute, and use a slotted spoon to transfer the squid to the ice bath.

2. Drain the squid, pat it dry, and set it aside.

3. Place the red wine vinegar, harissa, and mustard in a salad bowl and whisk to combine. While whisking, slowly drizzle in the olive oil until it has emulsified.

4. Add the chilled calamari, oranges, bell pepper, and celery and gently toss until combined.

5. Season the salad with salt and pepper, top with the hazelnuts and mint, and enjoy.

Spinach, Fennel & Apple Salad with Smoked Trout

YIELD: 4 Servings
ACTIVE TIME: 15 Minutes
TOTAL TIME: 15 Minutes

INGREDIENTS

2 tablespoons white wine vinegar

1 tablespoon fresh lemon juice

1 tablespoon grainy mustard

1 teaspoon honey

½ cup extra-virgin olive oil

1 shallot, minced

2 teaspoons chopped fresh tarragon

Salt and pepper, to taste

4 cups baby spinach

2 Granny Smith apples, halved, seeds removed, sliced thin

1 fennel bulb, trimmed, cored, and sliced thin

½ lb. smoked trout, skin removed, flaked

DIRECTIONS

1. Place the vinegar, lemon juice, mustard, and honey in a salad bowl and whisk to combine. While whisking continually, slowly drizzle in the olive oil until it has emulsified. Stir in the shallot and tarragon and season the vinaigrette with salt and pepper.

2. Add the spinach, apples, and fennel to the salad bowl and toss to coat.

3. To serve, plate the salad, top each portion with some of the smoked trout, and enjoy.

Fish & Chips

YIELD: 4 Servings
ACTIVE TIME: 15 Minutes
TOTAL TIME: 15 Minutes

INGREDIENTS

Canola oil, as needed

5 potatoes, sliced into long, thin strips

2 tablespoons chopped fresh rosemary

Salt, to taste

2 eggs, beaten

1 cup cornmeal

1½ lbs. pollock fillets

Lemon wedges, for serving

DIRECTIONS

1. Add canola oil to a Dutch oven until it is 2 inches deep and warm it to 350°F over medium-high heat. Place the sliced potatoes in the oil and fry until golden brown. Remove the fried potatoes with a slotted spoon and transfer to a paper towel-lined plate to drain.

2. Warm the oil back to 350°F. While the oil is warming, place the fried potatoes in a bowl, add the rosemary, season with salt, and toss to coat.

3. Place the beaten eggs in a small bowl and the cornmeal in another. Dredge the pollock fillets in the egg and then in the cornmeal, repeating until they are coated all over.

4. Place the battered pollock in the oil and fry until golden brown and cooked through, about 5 minutes.

5. Serve the fried fish with the fried potatoes and lemon wedges.

Crispy Salmon Rice

YIELD: 2 Servings
ACTIVE TIME: 15 Minutes
TOTAL TIME: 15 Minutes

INGREDIENTS

2 tablespoons avocado oil

½ white onion, minced

¼ cup sliced scallions

¼ cup chopped fresh parsley

2 teaspoons kosher salt

2 cups leftover white rice

6 oz. salmon belly, chopped

1 tablespoon pomegranate molasses

1 tablespoon apple cider vinegar

DIRECTIONS

1. Place the avocado oil in a large skillet and warm it over high heat. Add the onion, scallions, parsley, and salt and cook, stirring frequently, until the onion is translucent, about 2 minutes.

2. Add the rice and cook, stirring frequently, until the rice is crispy, about 3 minutes. Add the salmon, reduce the heat to medium-high, and cook until the salmon is cooked through, about 4 minutes.

3. Place the pomegranate molasses and vinegar in a small bowl and whisk to combine. Add this mixture to the pan and stir until incorporated.

4. Remove the pan from heat and enjoy immediately.

Crispy Salmon Rice, see page 129

Shrimp Cocktail, Baja Style

YIELD: 4 Servings
ACTIVE TIME: 15 Minutes
TOTAL TIME: 15 Minutes

DIRECTIONS

1. Place water in a medium saucepan, add the shrimp shells, lemon, salt, oregano, and bay leaves, and bring to a boil. Reduce the heat and simmer for 5 minutes.

2. While the broth is simmering, place the lime juice, lemon juice, orange juice, horseradish, ketchup, fish sauce, hot sauce, Clamato, and Worcestershire sauce in a mixing bowl and stir to combine.

3. Add the shrimp to the simmering broth and turn off the burner. Let the shrimp poach for 1 minute, remove it, and let it cool slightly.

4. Add the onion, garlic, avocado, jalapeños, tomatoes, and shrimp to the dressing and fold to incorporate. Garnish with cilantro and serve with lime wedges and tortillas.

INGREDIENTS

1 lb. shrimp, shells removed and reserved, deveined

1 lemon, halved

¼ cup kosher salt, plus more to taste

1 tablespoon dried Mexican oregano

2 bay leaves

7 tablespoons fresh lime juice

1½ tablespoons fresh lemon juice

5 tablespoons orange juice

1 tablespoon horseradish

14 tablespoons ketchup

1¼ tablespoons fish sauce

7 tablespoons hot sauce

7 tablespoons spicy Clamato

2⅔ tablespoons Worcestershire sauce

1 small red onion, sliced thin

5 garlic cloves, grated

Flesh of 1 avocado, diced

2 jalapeño chile peppers, stems and seeds removed, diced

2 tomatoes, diced

Fresh cilantro, chopped, for garnish

Lime wedges, for serving

Corn tortillas, for serving

Aguachile

YIELD: 4 Servings
ACTIVE TIME: 10 Minutes
TOTAL TIME: 15 Minutes

INGREDIENTS

1¾ cups fresh lime juice

3 serrano chile peppers, stems and seeds removed

1 cup fresh cilantro, chopped, plus more for garnish

3 tablespoons extra-virgin olive oil

2 tablespoons apple juice

1 teaspoon honey

Salt, to taste

1 lb. shrimp, shells removed, deveined

¼ red onion, sliced

1 cucumber, sliced

Flesh of 1 avocado, diced

Saltines, for serving

DIRECTIONS

1. Place the lime juice, serrano peppers, cilantro, olive oil, apple juice, and honey in a blender and puree until smooth. Season the aguachile with salt and set it aside.
2. Slice the shrimp in half lengthwise and place them in a shallow bowl. Cover with the red onion, cucumber, and avocado.
3. Pour the aguachile over the shrimp and let it cure for 5 to 7 minutes before garnishing with additional cilantro and serving with saltines.

Oysters with Juniper Cream

YIELD: 2 Servings
ACTIVE TIME: 15 Minutes
TOTAL TIME: 15 Minutes

INGREDIENTS

3 tablespoons unsalted butter, softened

2 oz. gin

1 teaspoon black pepper

¼ cup heavy cream

2 shallots, minced

4 juniper berries

Salt, as needed

12 oysters, shucked

Fresh parsley, chopped, for garnish

DIRECTIONS

1. Preheat your gas grill to high heat (about 500°F). Place the butter, gin, and black pepper in a bowl and whisk to combine. Set the mixture aside.

2. Place the cream, shallots, and juniper berries in a saucepan and warm over low heat for 2 minutes. Remove the pan from heat and let the mixture steep.

3. Fill a large cast-iron skillet with a bed of salt and nestle the oysters into the salt. Top each one with a spoonful of the butter mixture and a splash of the juniper cream.

4. Place the pan on the grill and cook until the oysters are caramelized and the liquid is bubbling, about 3 minutes.

5. Garnish with chopped parsley and serve immediately.

Honey-Glazed Salmon

YIELD: 4 Servings
ACTIVE TIME: 15 Minutes
TOTAL TIME: 15 Minutes

INGREDIENTS

4 skin-on salmon fillets, deboned

3 tablespoons extra-virgin olive oil

Salt, to taste

3 tablespoons honey

Zest and juice of 1 large lemon

DIRECTIONS

1. Pat the salmon fillets dry with a paper towel. Rub them with 1 tablespoon of the olive oil and season with salt.

2. Place a large cast-iron skillet over medium-high heat and add the remaining olive oil. Place the salmon fillets, skin side down, in the pan and cook for 5 minutes.

3. Reduce the heat to medium and use a spatula to carefully flip the salmon fillets over. Cook until they are cooked through and offer a little resistance when you squeeze the sides, 4 to 5 minutes.

4. While the salmon is cooking, place the honey, lemon zest, and lemon juice in a bowl and stir to combine.

5. Remove the salmon from the skillet, drizzle the honey glaze over the top, and enjoy.

Blackened Tilapia

YIELD: 4 Servings
ACTIVE TIME: 15 Minutes
TOTAL TIME: 15 Minutes

INGREDIENTS

2 tablespoons paprika

1 tablespoon onion powder

3 tablespoons garlic powder

2 tablespoons cayenne pepper

1½ teaspoons celery salt

1½ tablespoons black pepper

1 tablespoon dried thyme

1 tablespoon dried oregano

1 tablespoon chipotle chile powder

1 lb. boneless tilapia fillets

8 tablespoons unsalted butter, melted

Lemon wedges, for serving

DIRECTIONS

1. In a bowl, combine all the seasonings and set the mixture aside.
2. Warm a large cast-iron skillet over high heat. While the skillet is warming up, rinse the tilapia fillets and pat them dry with paper towels. Dip the fillets in the melted butter and then press some of the seasoning mixture into both sides.
3. Place the tilapia in the skillet and cook until the flesh is opaque and offers a little resistance when you squeeze the sides, 5 to 6 minutes.
4. Remove the tilapia from the pan, serve with lemon wedges, and enjoy.

Dogfish Chraime

YIELD: 2 Servings
ACTIVE TIME: 15 Minutes
TOTAL TIME: 15 Minutes

INGREDIENTS

2 tablespoons extra-virgin olive oil

½ onion, diced

2 garlic cloves, minced

3 tomatoes, diced

Pinch of cumin

Pinch of cayenne pepper

2 teaspoons kosher salt

¾ lb. dogfish fillet

1 teaspoon black pepper

DIRECTIONS

1. Place 1 tablespoon of the olive oil in a medium skillet and warm it over medium-high heat. Add the onion and garlic and cook, stirring frequently, until the onion is translucent, about 3 minutes.

2. Stir in the tomatoes, cumin, cayenne, and 1 teaspoon of the salt and bring the mixture to a simmer. Cook, stirring occasionally, until the tomatoes start to break down, about 5 minutes. Remove the pan from heat.

3. While the sauce is simmering, cut the fillet in half and season it with the pepper and remaining salt. Place the remaining olive oil in a clean skillet and warm it over high heat. Place the fish in the pan and cook until it is browned on both sides and cooked through, about 4 minutes, turning it over just once.

4. To serve, spoon some of the sauce into a shallow bowl, place the fish on top, and spoon a little more sauce over the top.

Dogfish Chraime, *see page 141*

Clams with Chorizo

YIELD: 4 to 6 Servings
ACTIVE TIME: 15 Minutes
TOTAL TIME: 15 Minutes

INGREDIENTS

24 littleneck clams, scrubbed well and rinsed

1 tablespoon extra-virgin olive oil

1 yellow onion, chopped

3 garlic cloves, minced

2 cups cherry tomatoes

2 oz. Spanish chorizo, minced

2 tablespoons unsalted butter, chopped

DIRECTIONS

1. Pick over the clams and discard any that are open, cracked, or damaged.
2. Place the olive oil in a 12-inch cast-iron skillet and warm it over medium heat. Add the onion and cook, without stirring, for 2 minutes. Add the garlic and tomatoes and cook, stirring occasionally, until the tomatoes start to collapse, about 5 minutes.
3. Add the chorizo, stir to incorporate, and cook for 2 minutes. Add the clams, cover the pot, and cook until the majority of the clams have opened, about 2 minutes.
4. Discard any clams that did not open. Add the butter to the pan, stir until it has melted, and serve.

Shrimp Curry

YIELD: 4 Servings
ACTIVE TIME: 15 Minutes
TOTAL TIME: 15 Minutes

DIRECTIONS

1. Place 4 of the shrimp, the coconut, cumin seeds, chiles de arbol, tomatoes, and canola oil in a food processor and puree into a paste.

2. Place the cloves, cardamom pods, bay leaves, and cinnamon stick in a large cast-iron skillet and toast the mixture over medium heat for 1 minute. Stir in the onion, coriander, turmeric, black pepper, garlic, and ginger. Cook for 1 minute, add the shrimp paste, and stir to combine. Cook, stirring frequently, for 3 minutes.

3. Add the coconut milk and water and bring to a boil. Add the brown sugar and serrano peppers, stir to incorporate, and cook for another minute.

4. Reduce the heat, add the remaining shrimp and the cilantro, and simmer until the shrimp are pink and the sauce thickens slightly, 2 to 4 minutes.

5. Season with salt and ladle the curry into warmed bowls.

INGREDIENTS

16 large shrimp, shells removed, deveined

1 cup unsweetened shredded coconut

1 teaspoon cumin seeds

3 chiles de arbol, stems removed

2 large tomatoes, chopped

¼ cup canola oil

5 whole cloves

4 green cardamom pods

2 bay leaves

1 cinnamon stick

1 yellow onion, chopped

1 tablespoon coriander

1 teaspoon turmeric

1 teaspoon black pepper

2 garlic cloves, mashed

1 teaspoon grated ginger

1 (14 oz.) can of coconut milk

½ cup water

2 tablespoons brown sugar

2 serrano chile peppers, stems and seeds removed, sliced thin

1 cup chopped fresh cilantro

Salt, to taste

One Step Ahead

When it comes down to it, planning ahead is the biggest component of getting dinner on the table quickly. Whether it be shopping or chopping, a little bit of preparation done over the weekend will help immensely when the time comes to get dinner on the table on a weeknight. These meals take that principle to its extreme, allowing the delicious things you make when you have a little more time to supply the foundation for memorable and speedy meals in the days that follow.

Roasted Chicken

YIELD: 8 to 10 Cups
ACTIVE TIME: 10 Minutes
TOTAL TIME: 1 Hour

INGREDIENTS

3 to 4 lb. whole chicken

Salt and pepper, to taste

DIRECTIONS

1. Preheat the oven to 450°F and place a cast-iron skillet in the oven as it warms. Rinse the chicken, inside and outside, and pat it dry with paper towels. This step is important because it ensures that the chicken roasts rather than steams.

2. Season with chicken generously, inside and outside, with salt and pepper. Put on oven mitts, remove the skillet from the oven, and place the chicken, breast side down, in the pan.

3. Place the pan in the oven and roast for 20 minutes. Reduce the oven's temperature to 350°F and roast until a meat thermometer inserted in the breast registers 165°F, about 35 minutes.

4. Remove from the oven, baste the chicken with the pan juices, and let it rest for 15 minutes before carving. Use the meat in one of the following preparations, toss it in pasta or a salad, or use as the basis of a sandwich.

Boiled Chicken

YIELD: 8 to 10 Cups
ACTIVE TIME: 15 Minutes
TOTAL TIME: 1 Hour

INGREDIENTS

3 to 4 lb. whole chicken

Salt and pepper, to taste

DIRECTIONS

1. Place the chicken in a large pot and cover with cold water. Add the salt and pepper and bring the water to a boil.

2. Cook the chicken until the meat is cooked through and tender, 40 minutes to 1 hour. If possible, the chicken should remain submerged for the entire time. If your pot is not large enough to guarantee this, carefully turn the chicken over occasionally to ensure that it cooks evenly. Use the meat in one of the following preparations, toss it in pasta or a salad, or use as the basis of a sandwich. Strain the cooking liquid and use it as chicken stock.

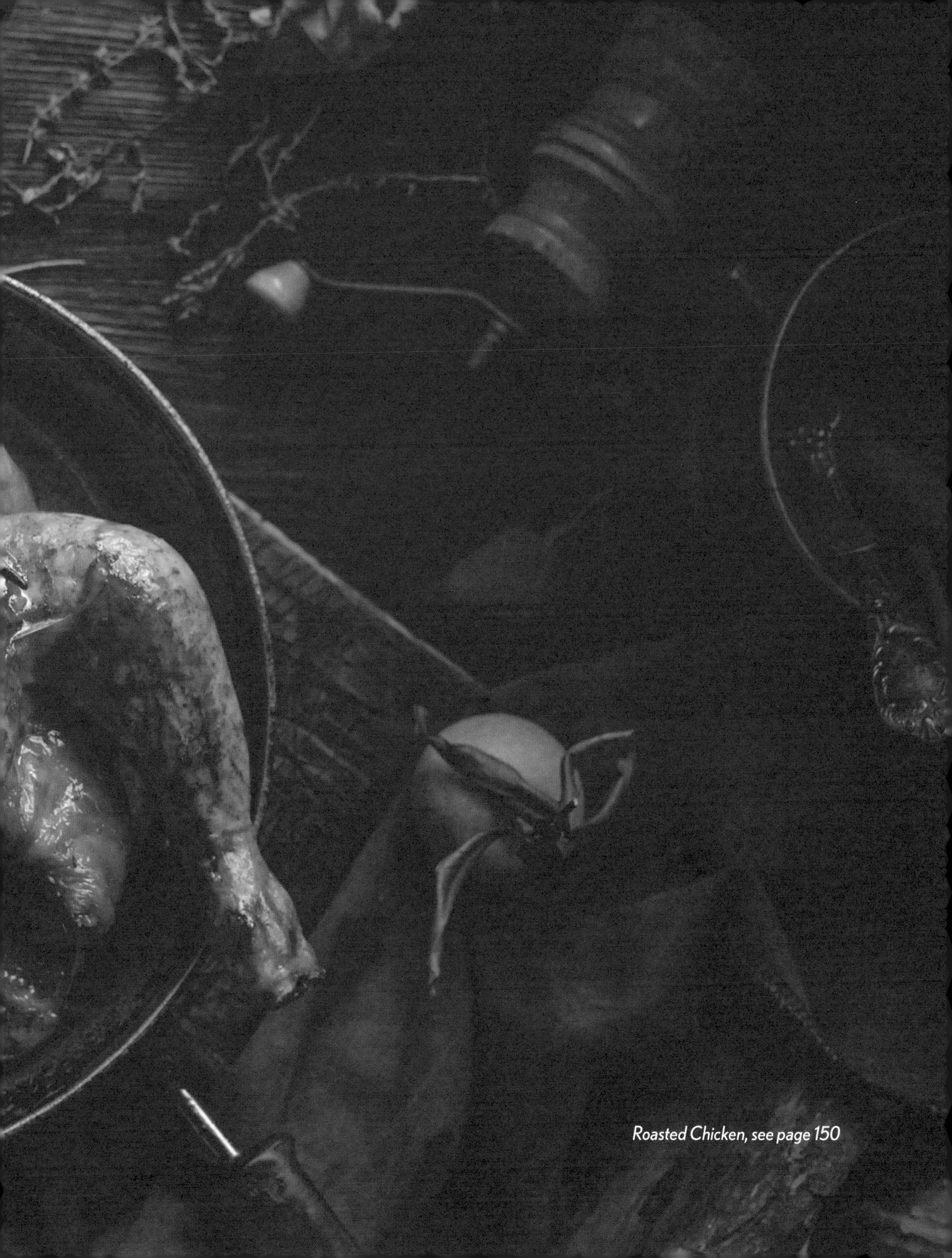

Roasted Chicken, see page 150

Classic Chicken Salad

YIELD: 4 to 6 Servings
ACTIVE TIME: 5 Minutes
TOTAL TIME: 5 Minutes

INGREDIENTS

$\frac{1}{3}$ cup mayonnaise

½ cup chopped celery

1 shallot, chopped

1 teaspoon mustard

½ teaspoon fresh lemon juice

4 cups shredded or diced leftover chicken (see page 150 or 151)

¼ cup walnuts or pecans

½ cup dried cranberries or halved seedless red grapes

Salt and pepper, to taste

Slices of sourdough bread or wraps, for serving

DIRECTIONS

1. Place the mayonnaise, celery, shallot, mustard, and lemon juice in a mixing bowl and stir to combine.

2. Add the chicken, walnuts, and dried cranberries and stir to incorporate. Season with salt and pepper and serve the chicken salad on the slices of sourdough or in wraps.

PB & C Sandwiches

YIELD: 4 Servings
ACTIVE TIME: 5 Minutes
TOTAL TIME: 5 Minutes

INGREDIENTS

¼ cup smooth peanut butter

8 slices of sourdough bread

1½ cups shredded leftover chicken (see page 150 or 151)

¼ cup shredded fresh basil

½ teaspoon kosher salt

DIRECTIONS

1. Spread the peanut butter over four slices of the bread. Top these slices with the chicken, basil, and salt and assemble the sandwiches using the remaining slices of bread.

Classic Chicken Salad, see page 154

Curried Chicken Salad

YIELD: 6 Servings
ACTIVE TIME: 5 Minutes
TOTAL TIME: 5 Minutes

INGREDIENTS

4 cups diced leftover chicken (see page 150 or 151)

¼ cup mayonnaise

3 tablespoons fresh lime juice

¼ cup Madras curry powder

1 tablespoon cumin

1 tablespoon garlic powder

½ teaspoon cinnamon

½ teaspoon turmeric

Salt and pepper, to taste

3 celery stalks, minced

2 Granny Smith apples, minced

½ red bell pepper, stem and seeds removed, minced

¾ cup pecans, chopped

3 oz. arugula

12 slices of marble rye, toasted

DIRECTIONS

1. Place the chicken, mayonnaise, lime juice, and the seasonings in a mixing bowl and stir to combine. Add the celery, apples, red pepper, and ½ cup of the pecans and stir to incorporate.

2. Add the arugula and toss to combine. Top with the remaining pecans and sandwich the chicken salad between the toasted slices of marble rye.

Pad Thai

YIELD: 4 to 6 Servings
ACTIVE TIME: 15 Minutes
TOTAL TIME: 15 Minutes

INGREDIENTS

6 oz. wide rice noodles

1 tablespoon avocado olive oil

1 large egg

3 cups shredded leftover chicken (see page 150 or 151)

¼ cup tamarind paste

2 tablespoons water

1½ tablespoons fish sauce

2 tablespoons rice vinegar

1½ tablespoons brown sugar

4 scallions, trimmed and sliced

1 cup bean sprouts

½ teaspoon cayenne pepper

¼ cup crushed peanuts

Lime wedges, for serving

DIRECTIONS

1. Place the noodles in a baking dish and cover with boiling water. Stir the noodles and then let them stand until they are tender, about 10 minutes. Drain and set them aside.

2. While the noodles are resting, place the avocado oil in a large wok or skillet and warm over medium-high heat. Add the egg and cook until it is almost set.

3. Add the chicken and stir to incorporate. While stirring to incorporate with every addition, add the tamarind paste, water, fish sauce, vinegar, brown sugar, scallions, bean sprouts, cayenne pepper, and peanuts.

4. Add the noodles, cook until everything is warmed through, and serve with the lime wedges.

BBQ Chicken Sandwiches

YIELD: 4 to 6 Servings
ACTIVE TIME: 5 Minutes
TOTAL TIME: 5 Minutes

INGREDIENTS

3 tablespoons mayonnaise, plus more to taste

1 tablespoon apple cider vinegar

¼ yellow onion, minced

2 tablespoons finely chopped fresh chives

2 cups shredded napa cabbage

Salt and pepper, to taste

2 to 3 cups shredded leftover chicken (see page 150 or 151)

½ cup barbecue sauce

4 to 6 brioche buns

DIRECTIONS

1. Place the mayonnaise, apple cider vinegar, onion, chives, and cabbage in a mixing bowl and stir to combine. Season with salt and pepper, add additional mayonnaise if desired, and set the slaw aside.

2. Place the chicken and barbecue sauce in a mixing bowl and stir to combine.

3. Spread some mayonnaise on the top halves of the brioche buns and set them aside. Place the dressed chicken on the bottom halves of the buns and top with some of the slaw. Assemble the sandwiches and serve.

Tinga de Pollo

YIELD: 6 Servings
ACTIVE TIME: 15 Minutes
TOTAL TIME: 15 Minutes

INGREDIENTS

1 tablespoon extra-virgin olive oil

1 white onion, sliced thin

1 garlic clove, sliced thin

3 large tomatoes, diced

2 cups shredded leftover chicken (see page 150 or 151)

2 chipotle chile peppers, stems and seeds removed, torn

Chicken Stock (see page 151), as needed

Salt, to taste

Corn tortillas, warm, for serving

Pickled red onion, for serving

DIRECTIONS

1. Place the olive oil in a large skillet and warm it over medium heat. Add the onion and garlic and cook, stirring frequently, until the onion is translucent, about 3 minutes.
2. Add the diced tomatoes and cook, stirring occasionally for another 5 minutes.
3. Add the chicken and chipotles and cook, stirring occasionally, until the flavor has developed to your liking, 4 to 5 minutes. Add stock to the pan if it starts looking too dry.
4. Season the dish with salt and serve with tortillas and pickled onion.

Tinga de Pollo, see page 163

Chicken Panini with Sun-Dried Tomato Aioli

YIELD: 4 Servings
ACTIVE TIME: 10 Minutes
TOTAL TIME: 10 Minutes

INGREDIENTS

For the Aioli

1 cup chopped sun-dried tomatoes

1 cup mayonnaise

1 tablespoon whole grain mustard

2 tablespoons finely chopped fresh parsley

2 tablespoons minced scallions

1 teaspoon white balsamic vinegar

1 garlic clove, minced

2 teaspoons kosher salt

1 teaspoon black pepper

For the Sandwiches

8 slices of crusty bread

8 slices of cheddar cheese

2 leftover chicken breasts (see page 150 or 151), sliced

12 slices of cooked bacon

1 cup arugula

DIRECTIONS

1. Preheat a panini press. To prepare the aioli, place all the ingredients in a mixing bowl and stir until combined.

2. To begin preparations for the sandwiches, spread some of the aioli on each slice of bread. Place a slice of cheddar on each slice of bread. Divide the chicken between four pieces of the bread. Top each portion of chicken with 3 slices of bacon and ¼ cup of the arugula and assemble the sandwiches.

3. Place the sandwiches in the panini press and press until the cheese has melted and there is a nice crust on the bread. Remove and serve immediately.

NOTE
If you don't have a panini press, don't worry. Simply place 1 tablespoon of olive oil in a large skillet and warm over medium-high heat. Place a sandwich in the pan, place a warmed cast-iron skillet on top so it is pressing down on the sandwich, and cook until golden brown. Turn the sandwich over and repeat.

Chicken Burritos

YIELD: 6 Servings
ACTIVE TIME: 15 Minutes
TOTAL TIME: 15 Minutes

INGREDIENTS

1 cup leftover white rice

¼ cup chopped fresh cilantro

1 (14 oz.) can of black beans, drained and rinsed

3 cups shredded leftover chicken (see page 150 or 151)

1 small red onion, chopped

2 tomatoes, diced

1 cup grated pepper jack cheese

6 large flour tortillas

Guacamole (see page 170), for serving

Salsa, for serving

Sour cream, for serving

DIRECTIONS

1. Place the rice in a bowl, stir in the cilantro, and set the mixture aside.

2. Layer the rice-and-cilantro mixture, beans, chicken, onion, tomatoes, and cheese on the tortillas. Wrap tightly and serve with Guacamole, salsa, and sour cream.

Guacamole

YIELD: 4 Servings
ACTIVE TIME: 10 Minutes
TOTAL TIME: 10 Minutes

INGREDIENTS

1 large tomato, finely diced

2 serrano chile peppers, finely diced

½ onion, finely diced

1 garlic clove, mashed

4 large avocados, pitted and diced

6 tablespoons fresh lime juice

Salt, to taste

½ cup fresh cilantro, chopped

DIRECTIONS

1. Combine the tomato, chiles, and onion in a bowl. Place the garlic clove in a separate bowl.
2. Add the avocado to the bowl containing the garlic and stir until well combined. Stir in the lime juice and season with salt.
3. Add the tomato mixture and stir until it has been incorporated. Add the cilantro and stir to combine. Taste and adjust the seasoning if necessary.

Chicken Caesar Salad

YIELD: 4 to 6 Servings
ACTIVE TIME: 5 Minutes
TOTAL TIME: 5 Minutes

INGREDIENTS

2 garlic cloves, chopped

½ cup extra-virgin olive oil

2 to 4 anchovies in olive oil, drained and chopped

2 tablespoons fresh lemon juice

Salt and pepper, to taste

4 romaine lettuce hearts, chopped

2 to 3 cups diced leftover chicken (see page 150 or 151)

¾ cup grated Parmesan cheese

Croutons, for garnish

DIRECTIONS

1. Place the garlic, olive oil, anchovies, and lemon juice in a food processor or blender and puree until smooth. Season with salt and pepper and set the dressing aside.

2. Place the lettuce in a salad bowl, add 2 to 3 tablespoons of the dressing, and toss to combine. Add the chicken, Parmesan, and remaining dressing and toss to combine. Garnish with the croutons and serve.

Chicken Fajitas

YIELD: 6 Servings
ACTIVE TIME: 15 Minutes
TOTAL TIME: 15 Minutes

INGREDIENTS

For the Chicken

½ cup orange juice

Juice of 1 lime

4 garlic cloves, minced

1 jalapeño chile pepper, stem and seeds removed, minced

2 tablespoons chopped fresh cilantro

1 teaspoon cumin

1 teaspoon dried oregano

Salt and pepper, to taste

3 tablespoons extra-virgin olive oil

6 cups sliced leftover chicken (see page 150 or 151)

For the Vegetables

2 tablespoons extra-virgin olive oil

1 red onion, sliced thin

3 bell peppers, stems and seeds removed, sliced thin

2 jalapeño chile peppers, stems and seeds removed, and sliced thin

Continued on page 174

DIRECTIONS

1. To begin preparations for the chicken, place the orange juice, lime juice, garlic, jalapeño, cilantro, cumin, oregano, salt, and pepper in a bowl and stir to combine. When thoroughly combined, add the olive oil. Add the chicken pieces to the mixture, stir until they are evenly coated and let stand for 10 minutes.

2. To prepare the vegetables, place the olive oil in a large cast-iron skillet and warm over medium heat. Add the onion, peppers, and garlic. Cook, while stirring, until the vegetables have softened, about 5 minutes. Add the lime juice and cilantro, season with salt and pepper, and cook until the vegetables are tender, about 10 minutes.

3. Push the vegetables to one side of the pan and put the chicken on the other side. Cook, while stirring, until the chicken is warmed through. Serve immediately with tortillas, Guacamole, and salsa.

3 garlic cloves, minced

¼ cup fresh lime juice

½ cup finely chopped fresh cilantro

Salt and pepper, to taste

Flour tortillas, for serving

Guacamole (see page 170), for serving

Salsa, for serving

Chicken Fajitas, see page 173

Chicken Tacos

YIELD: 6 Servings
ACTIVE TIME: 5 Minutes
TOTAL TIME: 5 Minutes

INGREDIENTS

4 cups chopped leftover chicken (see page 150 or 151)

1 tablespoon kosher salt

1 tablespoon cumin

1 tablespoon garlic powder

1 tablespoon cayenne pepper

½ red onion, sliced

Guacamole (see page 170), for serving

Corn or flour tortillas, for serving

DIRECTIONS

1. Place all of the ingredients, except for the Guacamole and tortillas, in a mixing bowl and toss to combine.

2. If desired, warm the dressed chicken in a skillet for 1 or 2 minutes. Serve with the Guacamole, tortillas, and other preferred taco fixings.

Chicken Tostadas

YIELD: 4 Servings
ACTIVE TIME: 15 Minutes
TOTAL TIME: 15 Minutes

INGREDIENTS

For the Tostadas

1 cup canola oil

½ cup corn kernels

1 small jalapeño chile pepper, stem and seeds removed, chopped, plus more for garnish

¼ cup minced red onion

2 teaspoons minced garlic

1½ tablespoons fresh lime juice

¼ cup finely chopped cilantro, plus more for garnish

½ cup chopped tomato

Salt and pepper, to taste

8 corn tortillas

Paprika, to taste

4 cups chopped or shredded leftover chicken (see page 150 or 151)

Red cabbage, shredded, for garnish

Continued on page 178

DIRECTIONS

1. To begin preparations for the tostadas, place the canola oil in a Dutch oven and warm to 350°F over medium-high heat. While the oil is warming up, place the corn, jalapeño, onion, garlic, lime juice, cilantro, and tomato in a mixing bowl and stir to combine. Season the mixture with salt and pepper and set aside.

2. Place the tortillas in the hot oil and fry until crispy. Remove from the oil, transfer to a paper towel–lined plate to drain, and season with salt and paprika.

3. To prepare the sour cream, place all the ingredients in a mixing bowl, stir to combine, and set aside.

4. Spread some sour cream on each tortilla and top with the corn salsa and chicken. Garnish with red cabbage and additional jalapeño and cilantro and serve with the lime wedges.

Lime wedges, for serving

For the Sour Cream

½ cup finely chopped fresh cilantro

¼ cup fresh lime juice

1¼ cups sour cream

1½ teaspoons kosher salt

½ teaspoon black pepper

Chicken Tacos, *see page 176*

Thai Chicken Salad

YIELD: 6 Servings
ACTIVE TIME: 15 Minutes
TOTAL TIME: 15 Minutes

DIRECTIONS

1. Bring water to a boil in a medium saucepan. To prepare the peanut sauce, place all the ingredients in a blender and puree until smooth. Set the sauce aside.

2. To begin preparations for the salad, add the noodles to the boiling water and briefly stir to prevent them from sticking together. Cook, while stirring, until the noodles are just tender, about 3 minutes. Drain, rinse with cold water, and let them drain further.

3. Place the noodles and the remaining ingredients in a salad bowl. Stir to combine, add the peanut sauce, toss to coat, and enjoy.

INGREDIENTS

For the Peanut Sauce

¼ cup fresh lime juice

2-inch piece of fresh ginger, peeled and grated

1 garlic clove

¼ cup brown sugar

2 tablespoons fish sauce

2 tablespoons soy sauce

½ cup smooth peanut butter

For the Salad

1 lb. rice stick noodles

½ lb. carrots, peeled and sliced thin

1 red bell pepper, stem and seeds removed, sliced thin

1 Fresno chile pepper, stem and seeds removed, sliced thin

2 jalapeño chile peppers, stems and seeds removed, sliced thin

4 scallions, trimmed and sliced thin

1 cup fresh basil leaves

¼ cup chopped fresh cilantro

2 tablespoons chopped fresh mint

4 cups diced leftover chicken (see page 150 or 151)

¼ cup roasted peanuts

Larb Gai

YIELD: 4 Servings
ACTIVE TIME: 15 Minutes
TOTAL TIME: 15 Minutes

INGREDIENTS

1 tablespoon avocado oil

1 shallot, minced

3 cups ground or minced leftover chicken (see page 150 or 151)

1 lemongrass stalk, minced

2 makrut lime leaves, minced

3 red chile peppers, stems and seeds removed, chopped

¼ cup fresh lime juice

1 tablespoon fish sauce

1 tablespoon soy sauce

¼ cup chopped fresh cilantro

12 fresh mint leaves, chopped

Salt and pepper, to taste

Bibb lettuce leaves, for serving

DIRECTIONS

1. Place a skillet over medium heat and add the avocado oil. Add the shallot and cook, stirring it occasionally, until it turns translucent, about 3 minutes.
2. Transfer the shallot to a bowl, add the ground chicken, lemongrass, lime leaves, chile peppers (if using), lime juice, fish sauce, soy sauce, cilantro, and mint, and stir to combine. Taste and season with salt and pepper.
3. Serve with the lettuce leaves, using them to scoop up the mixture.

TIP

Lemongrass and lime leaves can be very fibrous, so make sure they are both minced very fine.

Cashew Butter Chicken

YIELD: 4 Servings
ACTIVE TIME: 15 Minutes
TOTAL TIME: 15 Minutes

INGREDIENTS

½ teaspoon kosher salt, plus more to taste

½ teaspoon cayenne paper, plus more to taste

½ teaspoon brown sugar

½ teaspoon chili powder

3 cups shredded leftover chicken (see page 150 or 151)

⅓ cup cashew butter

¼ cup soy sauce

1½ tablespoons rice vinegar

2½ teaspoons toasted sesame oil

2 teaspoons chili oil

¾ teaspoon sugar

2 garlic cloves, minced

¾ lb. Chinese egg noodles

1 lb. Swiss chard, stems removed, leaves sliced into ribbons

6 scallions, trimmed and sliced thin

DIRECTIONS

1. Bring water to a boil in a medium saucepan. Place the salt, cayenne pepper, brown sugar, and chili powder in a mixing bowl and stir until well combined. Add the chicken and toss to coat.

2. Place the cashew butter, soy sauce, rice vinegar, sesame oil, chili oil, sugar, and garlic in a separate mixing bowl and stir until well combined.

3. Add salt and the noodles to the boiling water and cook for 1 minute.

4. Add the Swiss chard and cook until the noodles are tender but still chewy, another 2 minutes. Drain and transfer to a large bowl. Add the shredded chicken and the cashew butter mixture, toss to coat evenly, top with the scallions, and serve.

Larb Gai, see page 182

Chicken Curry

YIELD: 4 to 6 Servings
ACTIVE TIME: 15 Minutes
TOTAL TIME: 15 Minutes

INGREDIENTS

5 tablespoons green curry paste

3 cups diced leftover chicken (see page 150 or 151)

2 tablespoons avocado oil

2 yellow onions, peeled and sliced

2 red bell peppers, stems and seeds removed, sliced

3-inch piece of fresh ginger, peeled and mashed

1 garlic clove, mashed

1 (14 oz.) can of coconut milk

3 tablespoons fish sauce

1 tablespoon Madras curry powder

2 tablespoons finely chopped fresh basil, plus more for garnish

Fresh cilantro, finely chopped, for garnish

Lime wedges, for serving

DIRECTIONS

1. Place 2 tablespoons of the green curry paste and the chicken in a mixing bowl and stir until the chicken is evenly coated.

2. Place the avocado oil in a large cast-iron skillet and warm over medium-high heat. When the oil starts to shimmer, add the onions, peppers, ginger, and garlic and cook, stirring frequently, until the vegetables start to soften, about 5 minutes. Add the coconut milk and remaining green curry paste and cook for another 3 minutes.

3. Add the fish sauce, curry powder, basil, and chicken and stir to combine. Cook until everything is warmed through and ladle the curry into warmed bowls. Garnish each portion with cilantro and additional basil and serve with lime wedges.

Chicken & Eggplant Stir-Fry

YIELD: 4 Servings
ACTIVE TIME: 15 Minutes
TOTAL TIME: 15 Minutes

INGREDIENTS

4 lbs. eggplant, trimmed and peeled

2 tablespoons Shaoxing rice wine

1 tablespoon soy sauce

2 teaspoons toasted sesame oil

2 leftover chicken breasts (see page 150 or 151), sliced thin

2 tablespoons peanut oil

2 jalapeño chile peppers, stems and seeds removed, sliced thin

1 red bell pepper, stem and seeds removed, sliced thin

2 garlic cloves, minced

2 scallions, trimmed and chopped

Sesame seeds, for garnish

DIRECTIONS

1. Cut each eggplant into ¼-inch-thick rounds, then cut each round into ¼-inch-wide strips.
2. Whisk the rice wine, soy sauce, and sesame oil together in a medium bowl. Add the chicken and toss until evenly coated.
3. Place the oil in a large wok or skillet and warm over medium-high heat. Add the peppers and cook until they start to soften, about 3 minutes. Add the garlic and scallions and cook until they start to brown, about 2 minutes.
4. Add the chicken and eggplant to the pan and cook, stirring continually, until everything is warmed through, about 4 minutes. Garnish the dish with the sesame seeds and serve immediately.

Chicken Curry, see page 186

Chicken & Green Beans

YIELD: 4 Servings
ACTIVE TIME: 15 Minutes
TOTAL TIME: 15 Minutes

INGREDIENTS

1 tablespoon avocado oil, plus more as needed

1 lb. green beans, trimmed

2 tablespoons kimchi, chopped

1 garlic clove, chopped

2 tablespoons Shaoxing rice wine

2 cups shredded leftover chicken (see page 150 or 151)

2 tablespoons soy sauce

1 tablespoon fermented black bean garlic sauce

1 teaspoon sugar

DIRECTIONS

1. Place the avocado oil in a wok or a large skillet and warm it over high heat. Add the green beans and let them sear on one side, undisturbed, for 4 minutes.

2. Stir the beans and add the kimchi and the garlic to the pan. Cook, stirring continuously, until the contents of the pan are fragrant, about 1 minute.

3. Add the rice wine and cook until it is nearly evaporated, about 3 minutes. Add the chicken, soy sauce, fermented black bean garlic sauce, and sugar and stir to incorporate. Cook until everything is warmed through and enjoy.

Chicken Chili

YIELD: 4 to 6 Servings
ACTIVE TIME: 15 Minutes
TOTAL TIME: 15 Minutes

DIRECTIONS

1. Place the olive oil in a large saucepan and warm over medium-high heat. Add the onion and cook, stirring occasionally, until it is translucent, about 3 minutes.

2. Add the garlic and cook, stirring continually, for 1 minute. Add the remaining ingredients, except for those designated for serving, and stir to combine. Bring the chili to a simmer and cook until the chili has thickened and the taste is to your liking, 8 to 10 minutes.

3. Season with salt and pepper, remove the aromatics and discard them, and ladle the chili into warmed bowls. Serve with the cheddar cheese, sour cream, and chives.

INGREDIENTS

1 tablespoon extra-virgin olive oil

1 yellow onion, chopped

2 garlic cloves, minced

1 tablespoon chili powder

1 bay leaf

2 sprigs of fresh thyme

2 sprigs of fresh parsley

4 cups diced or shredded leftover chicken (see page 150 or 151)

4 tomatoes, diced

2 cups tomato sauce

½ cup tomato paste

2 cups canned corn

1 (14 oz.) can of kidney beans, drained and rinsed

1 (14 oz.) can of cannellini beans, drained and rinsed

1 (14 oz.) can of black beans, drained and rinsed

Salt and pepper, to taste

Cheddar cheese, shredded, for serving

Sour cream, for serving

Fresh chives, finely chopped, for serving

Avgolemono

YIELD: 4 Servings
ACTIVE TIME: 15 Minutes
TOTAL TIME: 15 Minutes

INGREDIENTS

6 cups Chicken Stock (see page 151)

½ cup orzo

3 eggs

1 tablespoon fresh lemon juice

1½ cups diced leftover chicken (see page 150 or 151)

Salt and pepper, to taste

Lemon slices, for garnish

Fresh dill, finely chopped, for garnish

DIRECTIONS

1. Place the stock in a saucepan and bring it to a boil. Reduce heat so that the stock simmers, add the orzo, and cook for 5 minutes.

2. Strain the stock and orzo over a large bowl. Set the orzo aside. Return the stock to the pan and bring to a simmer.

3. Place the eggs in a mixing bowl and beat until scrambled. Add the lemon juice and whisk to incorporate. While stirring constantly, add approximately ½ cup of the stock to the mixture. Stir another cup of stock into the egg mixture and then stir the tempered eggs into the saucepan. Be careful not to let the stock come to boil once you add the egg mixture.

4. Stir the chicken and orzo into the soup and cook until warmed through, about 2 minutes. Season with salt and pepper, ladle into warmed bowls, and garnish with lemon slices and dill.

Chicken Succotash Soup

YIELD: 4 to 6 Servings
ACTIVE TIME: 15 Minutes
TOTAL TIME: 15 Minutes

INGREDIENTS

4 tablespoons unsalted butter

4 slices of thick-cut bacon, chopped

2 onions, chopped

2 garlic cloves, minced

¼ cup all-purpose flour

4 cups Chicken Stock (see page 151)

2 to 3 cups diced leftover chicken (see page 150 or 151)

2 cups canned corn

1 (14 oz.) can of kidney beans, drained and rinsed

1 cup heavy cream

3 tablespoons finely chopped fresh parsley

Salt and pepper, to taste

DIRECTIONS

1. Place the butter in a large saucepan and melt it over medium heat. Add the bacon, onions, and garlic and cook until the bacon starts to brown and the onions start to soften, about 5 minutes.
2. Add the flour and cook, stirring constantly, for 2 minutes. Gradually add the stock and whisk constantly to prevent lumps from forming. Bring to a boil and then add the chicken, corn kernels, and kidney beans. Reduce the heat and simmer for 3 minutes.
3. Stir in the cream and return the soup to a simmer. Add chopped parsley, season with salt and pepper, and ladle the soup into warmed bowls.

Roasted Eggplants

YIELD: 8 Cups
ACTIVE TIME: 5 Minutes
TOTAL TIME: 45 Minutes

INGREDIENTS

2 eggplants

Salt, to taste

Extra-virgin olive oil, to taste

DIRECTIONS

1. Preheat the oven to 400°F.

2. Score the eggplants with a knife, season them with salt, and drizzle some olive oil over them. Rub the salt and olive oil into the flesh, place the eggplants on a baking sheet, cut side down, and place them in the oven.

3. Roast the eggplants until they have collapsed, 35 to 45 minutes. Remove the eggplants from the oven and let them cool. Use in one of the following preparations, to top Crostini (see page 26), in a salad, as the base a soup, or toss it with pasta and other vegetables.

Baba Ghanoush

YIELD: 12 Servings
ACTIVE TIME: 5 Minutes
TOTAL TIME: 5 Minutes

INGREDIENTS

2 Roasted Eggplants (see page 198)

4 garlic cloves, smashed

4 teaspoons fresh lemon juice, plus more to taste

1½ teaspoons kosher salt, plus more to taste

½ cup tahini paste

¼ cup pomegranate seeds

2 teaspoons finely chopped fresh parsley

¼ cup extra-virgin olive oil

Pita bread, for serving

DIRECTIONS

1. Scoop the flesh of the eggplants into a food processor and discard the skins. Add the garlic, lemon juice, salt, and tahini and blitz until the mixture is smooth and creamy, about 1 minute. Taste and add more lemon juice and salt as necessary.

2. Transfer the baba ghanoush to a bowl, top with the pomegranate seeds, parsley, and olive oil, and serve with pita bread.

Baba Ghanoush, see page 199

Caponata

YIELD: 6 Servings
ACTIVE TIME: 15 Minutes
TOTAL TIME: 15 Minutes

INGREDIENTS

2 tablespoons extra-virgin olive oil

1 onion, chopped

2 celery stalks, peeled and chopped

3 large garlic cloves, minced

2 red bell peppers, stems and seeds removed, chopped

Salt and pepper, to taste

1 Roasted Eggplant (see page 198), chopped

1 (14 oz.) can of crushed tomatoes, with their liquid

2 tablespoons plus 1 pinch sugar

3 tablespoons (heaping) capers, rinsed and drained

3 tablespoons chopped green olives

3 tablespoons red wine vinegar

DIRECTIONS

1. Place 1 tablespoon of the oil in a large skillet and warm it over medium-high heat. Add the onion and celery and cook, stirring frequently, until the onion starts to soften, about 3 minutes. Stir in the garlic and peppers, season the dish with salt and cook, stirring frequently, until the peppers are tender, about 6 minutes.

2. Stir in the eggplant, tomatoes, sugar, capers, olives, and vinegar and cook until the mixture has thickened, about 5 minutes. Remove the pan from heat and enjoy immediately, or let the caponata cool in the refrigerator overnight.

Roasted Eggplant Pita

YIELD: 6 Servings
ACTIVE TIME: 10 Minutes
TOTAL TIME: 10 Minutes

INGREDIENTS

3 tablespoons extra-virgin olive oil

2 garlic cloves, minced

1 Roasted Eggplant (see page 198), chopped

1 cup cherry tomatoes, halved

3 pickle spears, sliced thin

⅓ cup chopped red onion

1 scallion, trimmed and sliced thin

¼ cup artichoke hearts

1 tablespoon chopped fresh parsley

1 teaspoon za'atar

Pita bread, for serving

Hummus, for serving

Poached eggs, for serving

Full-fat Greek yogurt, for serving

DIRECTIONS

1. Place 1 tablespoon of the olive oil in a large saucepan and warm it over medium heat. Add the garlic and cook, stirring continually, until it is fragrant, about 1 minute.
2. Place the garlic in a bowl, add the eggplant, tomatoes, pickles, onion, scallion, artichokes, parsley, za'atar, and remaining olive oil and stir to combine.
3. Build your desired sandwich from the eggplant-and-tomato mixture and any or all of the remaining ingredients.

Turkish Eggplant Salad

YIELD: 4 Servings
ACTIVE TIME: 15 Minutes
TOTAL TIME: 15 Minutes

INGREDIENTS

2 tablespoons extra-virgin olive oil

3 tomatoes, diced

1 white onion, julienned

2 Roasted Eggplants (see page 198)

4 garlic cloves, minced

1 tablespoon paprika

1 teaspoon kosher salt

1 teaspoon cumin

1 teaspoon cayenne pepper

½ cup chopped fresh parsley

DIRECTIONS

1. Place the olive oil in a large skillet and warm it over medium-high heat. Add the tomatoes and onion and cook until the onion is translucent, about 3 minutes. Add the remaining ingredients, except for the parsley, and cook about 6 minutes, stirring occasionally.

2. Transfer the mixture to a serving dish, stir in the parsley, and either enjoy immediately or chill the salad in the refrigerator overnight.

Eggplant & Zucchini Soup

YIELD: 4 Servings
ACTIVE TIME: 15 Minutes
TOTAL TIME: 15 Minutes

INGREDIENTS

1 Roasted Eggplant (see page 198), peeled and chopped

2 large zucchini, chopped

1 onion, chopped

3 garlic cloves, minced

2 tablespoons extra-virgin olive oil

1 tablespoon finely chopped fresh oregano

1 tablespoon chopped fresh mint

2 cups heavy cream

Salt and pepper, to taste

Crème fraîche, for garnish

DIRECTIONS

1. Place the eggplant, zucchini, onion, garlic, olive oil, oregano, and mint in a food processor and blitz until the mixture is smooth.

2. Place the puree in a medium saucepan, stir in the heavy cream, and bring the soup to a simmer.

3. Season the soup with salt and pepper, ladle it into warmed bowls, and garnish each portion with crème fraîche.

Braised Beef

YIELD: 6 Servings
ACTIVE TIME: 10 Minutes
TOTAL TIME: 1½ to 2½ Hours

INGREDIENTS

2 lbs. beef chuck or brisket, trimmed

Salt, to taste

3 garlic cloves, smashed

2 bay leaves

2 sprigs of fresh thyme

½ onion, chopped

1 teaspoon dried oregano

DIRECTIONS

1. Season the beef with salt and place it in a large saucepan. Cover it with water and bring it to a simmer over medium heat.

2. Using a piece of cheesecloth, create a sachet with the garlic, bay leaves, thyme, onion, and oregano. Secure the sachet with kitchen twine and add it to the saucepan.

3. Simmer the beef until it is very tender, just shy of falling apart, 1 to 2 hours. Remove the pan from heat and let the meat cool in the broth.

4. Remove the beef from the broth and use in one of the following preparations, in a sauce or soup, or pile it on bread and make a sandwich. Strain the broth and use it as a stock for soup or chili.

Beef Ramen

YIELD: 4 Servings
ACTIVE TIME: 15 Minutes
TOTAL TIME: 15 Minutes

INGREDIENTS

3 to 4 cups Beef Stock (see opposite page)

2 teaspoons rice vinegar

1 tablespoon honey

1 teaspoon fish sauce

4 oz. oyster mushrooms

4 oz. ramen noodles

1 lb. Braised Beef (see opposite page), sliced thin

DIRECTIONS

1. Place the stock in a saucepan and bring it to a boil.

2. Stir in the vinegar, honey, fish sauce, mushrooms, and noodles and cook until the noodles are just shy of al dente, about 4 minutes.

3. Stir in the beef, cook until it is warmed through, and ladle the ramen into bowls.

Beef Ramen, see page 211

Beef & Broccoli

YIELD: 4 Servings
ACTIVE TIME: 15 Minutes
TOTAL TIME: 15 Minutes

INGREDIENTS

1 tablespoon avocado oil

2 garlic cloves, minced

1 lb. broccoli, cut into florets

¼ cup thinly sliced eggplant

¼ cup oyster sauce

1 tablespoon soy sauce

1 lb. Braised Beef (see page 210), shredded

Chile peppers, sliced thin, for garnish

DIRECTIONS

1. Coat a large skillet or wok with avocado oil and warm it over high heat. Add the garlic, broccoli, and eggplant and cook, stirring frequently, until the broccoli has softened and the eggplant has collapsed, about 7 minutes.

2. Add the oyster sauce, soy sauce, and beef and cook until the beef is warmed through and the broccoli is tender, about 4 minutes. Garnish with the chile peppers and enjoy.

Dzik de Res

YIELD: 6 Servings
ACTIVE TIME: 15 Minutes
TOTAL TIME: 15 Minutes

INGREDIENTS

2 lbs. Braised Beef (see page 210), shredded

1 cup fresh lime juice

1 cup orange juice

Salt, to taste

3 oz. radishes, sliced thin

3 habanero chile peppers, stems and seeds removed, minced

1 large red onion, julienned

2 avocados, pitted and sliced

½ lb. Roma tomatoes, seeded and chopped

1 small bunch of fresh cilantro, chopped

Corn tortillas, warm, for serving

Lime wedges, for serving

DIRECTIONS

1. Place the beef in a mixing bowl, add the lime juice and orange juice, and stir to combine. Season the mixture with salt and then fold in the radish, habanero, red onion, avocados, tomatoes, and cilantro.

2. Serve with tortillas and lime wedges.

Avikas

YIELD: 6 Servings
ACTIVE TIME: 15 Minutes
TOTAL TIME: 15 Minutes

INGREDIENTS

1 tablespoon extra-virgin olive oil

1 yellow onion, chopped

1 tablespoon tomato paste

1 lb. Braised Beef (see page 210), chopped

½ cup canned cannellini beans

1 tablespoon kosher salt

¼ teaspoon black pepper

DIRECTIONS

1. Place the olive oil in a large saucepan and warm it over medium-high heat. Add the onion to the pan and cook, stirring occasionally, until it has softened, about 5 minutes. Add the tomato paste and cook until it has caramelized, about 2 minutes.

2. While the onion is cooking, place the beef and beans in a saucepan, cover the mixture with water, and stir in the salt and pepper. Bring the mixture to a simmer.

3. Stir in the onion-and-tomato paste mixture, ladle the soup into warmed bowls, and enjoy.

Roasted Squash

YIELD: 2 to 3 Cups
ACTIVE TIME: 5 Minutes
TOTAL TIME: 1 Hour

INGREDIENTS

1 squash, such as butternut, acorn, summer, Blue Hubbard

Salt, to taste

Extra-virgin olive oil, to taste

DIRECTIONS

1. Preheat the oven to 400°F. Halve the squash, scoop out any seeds, and season the squash with salt. Drizzle olive oil over the squash, place it on a baking sheet, cut side down, and place it in the oven.

2. Roast the squash until it is soft enough that a knife easily passes through the flesh when it is inserted. The time needed will vary depending on the size and variety of squash, but plan on a medium butternut or acorn squash taking around 40 minutes.

3. Remove the squash from the oven and let it cool. When the squash is cool enough to handle, slice the flesh and leave it as is, or mash it. Use in one of the following preparations, in a salad, as the base of a soup, spread over Crostini (see page 26), or toss it with pasta and other vegetables.

Stuffed Avocados

YIELD: 2 Servings
ACTIVE TIME: 15 Minutes
TOTAL TIME: 15 Minutes

INGREDIENTS

2 ripe avocados

½ cup crumbled feta cheese

1 cup roasted and diced butternut squash (see opposite page)

Salt and pepper, to taste

1 tablespoon extra-virgin olive oil

DIRECTIONS

1. Preheat the oven to 400°F. Halve the avocados and remove their seeds. Scoop the flesh of the avocados into a bowl. Add the feta and roasted squash and mash the mixture until it is smooth and well combined. Season the mixture with salt and pepper.

2. Fill the avocado skins with the mixture and lightly brush the top of each one with some of the olive oil. Place the stuffed avocados on a baking sheet and place them in the oven.

3. Roast in the oven until the tops of the avocado are browned, about 10 minutes. Remove from the oven and enjoy.

Stuffed Avocados, see page 221

Squash & Feta Salad

YIELD: 4 Servings
ACTIVE TIME: 10 Minutes
TOTAL TIME: 10 Minutes

INGREDIENTS

¼ cup sherry vinegar

1 teaspoon honey

1 teaspoon fresh thyme

¼ cup avocado oil

½ teaspoon kosher salt

½ teaspoon sweet Hungarian paprika

½ teaspoon cayenne pepper

1 head of radicchio, leaves separated and torn into large pieces

Roasted Squash (see page 220), chopped

½ lb. feta cheese, crumbled

DIRECTIONS

1. Place the vinegar, honey, thyme, avocado oil, and salt in a large bowl and whisk until thoroughly combined.
2. In a small bowl, combine the paprika and cayenne and set the mixture aside.
3. Add the radicchio and squash to the dressing and toss to coat.
4. Sprinkle the feta and paprika-and-cayenne blend over the salad and enjoy.

Butternut Squash & Chorizo Bisque

YIELD: 4 Servings
ACTIVE TIME: 15 Minutes
TOTAL TIME: 15 Minutes

INGREDIENTS

Roasted butternut squash (see page 220)

1 onion, sliced

1 cup heavy cream

1 cup Chicken Stock (see page 151)

1 cup whole milk

2 bay leaves

1 tablespoon extra-virgin olive oil

½ lb. chorizo, casing removed

4 tablespoons unsalted butter

DIRECTIONS

1. Place the squash, onion, cream, stock, and milk in a blender and puree until it is smooth.
2. Place the puree in a saucepan, add the bay leaves, and bring the soup to a simmer.
3. While the soup is coming to a simmer, place the olive oil in a skillet and warm it over medium-high heat. Add the chorizo and cook, turning as needed, until the chorizo is browned, about 5 minutes. Chop the chorizo and place it in a bowl.
4. Stir in the butter into the soup, remove the bay leaves, and discard them.
5. Ladle the soup into warmed bowls, top each portion with some of the chorizo, and enjoy.

Roasted Beets

YIELD: 2 Cups
ACTIVE TIME: 15 Minutes
TOTAL TIME: 2 Hours

INGREDIENTS

3 to 4 beets

Extra-virgin olive oil, to taste

DIRECTIONS

1. Preheat the oven to 425°F. Trim the beets to remove their stems. Rinse the beets well, place them in a baking dish, and drizzle olive oil over them.

2. Cover the baking dish with aluminum foil, place it in the oven, and roast the beets until a knife passes easily through to the center when inserted.

3. Remove the beets from the oven and let them cool. When the beets are cool enough to handle, peel and dice them. Use in one of the following preparations, in a salad, or as the base of a soup.

Beets with Walnut Dukkah

YIELD: 2 Servings
ACTIVE TIME: 15 Minutes
TOTAL TIME: 15 Minutes

INGREDIENTS

1 tablespoon chopped walnuts

1 tablespoon chopped hazelnuts

Pinch of kosher salt

1 teaspoon black pepper

1 teaspoon poppy seeds

1 teaspoon black sesame seeds

1 tablespoon avocado oil

Roasted Beets (see opposite page)

¼ cup full-fat Greek yogurt

1 cinnamon stick

DIRECTIONS

1. Place the nuts in a resealable bag and use a rolling pin to crush them. Transfer to a small bowl, add the salt, black pepper, and seeds, and stir to combine.

2. Place the avocado oil in a large skillet and warm it over high heat. Place the beets in the pan and sear until well browned all over, about 5 minutes, turning the beets as necessary.

3. To serve, spread the yogurt across a shallow bowl, pile the beets on top, and sprinkle the dukkah over the dish. Grate the cinnamon stick over the top of the dish until it is to your taste and enjoy.

Beets with Walnut Dukkah, *see page 229*

Strawberry & Beet Salad

YIELD: 4 Servings
ACTIVE TIME: 5 Minutes
TOTAL TIME: 5 Minutes

INGREDIENTS

Roasted Beets (see page 228), diced

Pesto (see page 49)

12 strawberries, hulled and halved

2 cups shredded fresh mozzarella cheese

4 oz. baby arugula

2 tablespoons extra-virgin olive oil

Salt and pepper, to taste

DIRECTIONS

1. Place the beets in a salad bowl with the Pesto and toss to coat.
2. Add the strawberries, mozzarella, arugula, and olive oil and toss until evenly distributed. Season the salad with salt and pepper and enjoy.

METRIC CONVERSIONS

US Measurement	Approximate Metric Liquid Measurement	Approximate Metric Dry Measurement
1 teaspoon	5 ml	5 g
1 tablespoon or ½ ounce	15 ml	14 g
1 ounce or ⅛ cup	30 ml	29 g
¼ cup or 2 ounces	60 ml	57 g
⅓ cup	80 ml	76 g
½ cup or 4 ounces	120 ml	113 g
⅔ cup	160 ml	151 g
¾ cup or 6 ounces	180 ml	170 g
1 cup or 8 ounces or ½ pint	240 ml	227 g
1½ cups or 12 ounces	350 ml	340 g
2 cups or 1 pint or 16 ounces	475 ml	454 g
3 cups or 1½ pints	700 ml	680 g
4 cups or 2 pints or 1 quart	950 ml	908 g

Index

D

E

F

G

About Cider Mill Press Book Publishers

Good ideas ripen with time. From seed to harvest, Cider Mill Press brings fine reading, information, and entertainment together between the covers of its creatively crafted books. Our Cider Mill bears fruit twice a year, publishing a new crop of titles each spring and fall.

CIDER MILL PRESS

BOOK PUBLISHERS

"Where Good Books Are Ready for Press"

Visit us online at
cidermillpress.com
or write to us at
PO Box 454
12 Spring St.
Kennebunkport, Maine 04046